WARRIOR APPRENTICESHIP
WITH THE
GRANDMASTER

Michael Coleman, Kyoshi

Editorial Supervision
by Grandmaster Shoto Tanemura

ACKNOWLEDGEMENTS

This book is dedicated to my teacher, Tanemura Sensei, without whose tireless efforts and infinite patience the true Amatsu Tatara tradition would have died out decades ago. He taught me the meaning of perseverance and humility. Also it is dedicated to my students and martial arts friends (past, present and future), who have and will carry the torch in ways yet to be discovered. Special thanks goes to David Herrell whose intuitive eye is responsible for most of the pictures captured in this book. In addition, my sincere gratitude goes out to the amazing Mr. Paul Gilmore who crafted the photograph featured on the front cover.

TABLE OF CONTENTS

SHIN DAI (SINCERE TRUST) BETWEEN TEACHER AND
STUDENT CAN ONLY BE DEVELOPED AFTER MANY
CONTINUOUS YEARS OF TRAINING UNDER THE MASTER

PREFACE

"What are the martial arts? - This is the most mysterious point which one gains without learning." These cryptic words were spoken by one of the greatest martial artists of the twentieth century, Grandmaster Takamatsu Toshitsugu*. He passed away in 1972, the same year I began studying martial arts.

I was too young to question why I liked the training. My family members had been soldiers for generations, and my uncle was even stationed in Asia and studied budo (Japanese martial arts). I guess it follows that my parents' daycare center curriculum included karate for Kindergarteners.

But as I grew older and after years of fighting in tournaments, my curiosity about the roots and true meaning behind the discipline grew. At fourteen, I stopped sparring and turned to more substantial forms of research and exercise.

Shortly after, I happened to pick up a book written by an American who had gone to Japan and trained with a mysterious master called Tanemura Sensei. The author was greatly impressed but for some reason missed his opportunity to complete his training with Tanemura Sensei.

Perhaps I had a chance...

I was only from a small city in the Midwest. I had no connection to the Japanese Grandmaster thousands of miles away. Even so I felt that somehow, I'd eventually meet Tanemura Sensei and receive the direct teaching I longed for.

Five years of searching went by, and because the internet had not yet been invented, the hunt was even more challenging. I was sometimes overcome by confusion and despair. At times, I even forgot the goal entirely. But eventually destiny reminded me that I had to learn the truth.

This book contains the story of how my apprenticeship unfolded. It was written at the request of Grandmaster Tanemura for several reasons. Quoted from Sensei:

1. **"These are true things."** All of the stories are factual not allegorical, and most happened in the presence of multiple witnesses.

2. **"Michael, it was never your mission to live in Japan."** Because of family obligations in the US, I never stayed overseas for much longer than a month at a time. Perhaps this doesn't sound as romantic as moving there indefinitely. But, my teacher observed from the beginning that for most people, relocation is an improbable dream. Tanemura Sensei wants my story to help those he cannot teach personally to understand it's possible to master this art from a distance.

3. **"Students need to learn the proper manners."** In Japan, etiquette is very important and loyalty to your teacher is absolute. In Chapter V, I recall a time when I was almost kicked out of the school for a violation of manners and loyalty. Originally, my lack of good judgment seemed innocent enough, but there are times when ignorance is not an acceptable excuse.

4. **"Tell them about how hard it was in the old days."** Before 1990, Tanemura Sensei's teaching method was more severe. I've also trained with people who knew the Grandmaster in the 1970's. Because he was a police detective back then, he never chose to charge his students. However, I was informed that they compensated him by offering their bodies for testing various locks, throws and pressure points – all of which were done to the limits of their endurance. These days the Grandmaster takes a more gentle approach. Yet, as a martial artist, Tanemura Sensei is even more powerful.

As you read these pages please understand that my apprenticeship is nowhere near finished. I have watched my teacher grow ever better over the years, and if anything, he has taught me to respect the ever-expanding potential in all of us. All I can say is that I have experienced enough to write my part in this story. Most of the other ideas were composed by several grandmasters years, or even centuries before I was born.

To develop as martial artists and human beings, we need honesty, patience and positive role models. Missing any one of these, our efforts will amount to nothing.

Takamatsu Sensei asked, "What are the martial arts?"

My hope is that this book inspires you to find out the only way possible: by training hard.

* Please notice that throughout the book, I write the Japanese names in a way that is proper in Japan: family name, given name and title.

Disclaimer: The reader should consult a physician before engaging in any form of strenuous physical activity like martial arts. To avoid unnecessary risks, nothing in this book should be attempted without the guidance and instruction of a qualified Genbukan instructor.

SHODAN

"To subdue the enemy without fighting
is the highest skill."
-Sun Tzu

CHAPTER I

MEETING TANEMURA SENSEI BY ACCIDENT

We were driving behind a gigantic truck when a wave of water splashed up from the road and crashed into my windshield. The wipers had to work extra hard, but eventually I could make out the yellow lines in the road.

It was the summer of 1987; the rain was coming down in buckets on Highway 80/90. To make matters worse, every semi-truck that passed me left a blinding wake of water behind its wheels. My friend Tim was asleep in the passenger seat. He had already concluded his half of the seven-hour drive to Ohio.

Then, I saw a wonderful thing. The sun had graciously decided to make an appearance up ahead. Just when I thought that things were clearing up for good, I caught something out the corner of my left eye. It disappeared quickly.

Between the two sides of the highway was a deep ditch. Perhaps, a State Trooper had stealthily parked his car and was waiting for a speeder.

"Crunch!" I didn't have time to wonder anymore. For a moment I lost control of the vehicle. In an instant, the car's radiator was bent inward at a forty-five-degree angle. The hood was crushed, and my wipers started to spread dark red blood evenly across the glass.

Luckily, no semi-trucks were thundering next to me anymore. I didn't know for sure though, because I was driving totally blind. When finally, I stopped moving, we were stranded on the side of the road. - In the 1980's, I did not own a cell phone.

Tim awakened violently and was understandably disoriented. His panicked stream of questions fell on deaf ears. I was replaying what had happened in my mind. Somehow, I was able to see it all in slow motion.

A female deer had left the woods and run into the road. Across the westbound side she had great success, managing to make it through three lanes of traffic without even the honk of a horn. That was what I had seen in my peripheral vision, but it didn't register until after the crash. The sun coming out from behind the clouds at that moment made it impossible for me to see her.

We were on our way to see a *Ninpo* (the source of ancient Japanese martial arts) grandmaster. At that time, we didn't know exactly who that would be. Tanemura Sensei was actually substitute teaching for a different Grandmaster.

Fate intervened, and we survived the collision. And, it was miraculous that I was able to complete the journey and accidentally meet Grandmaster Shoto Tanemura in person.

HAJIME MASHITE!

Sensei was a striking figure in his traditional *samue* (Japanese casual suit). It was cobalt blue with a white under-kimono. The fine material was in stark contrast to the simple black or white karate uniforms worn by his audience. I later learned that his luggage had been lost and he was forced to train in his "street clothes". No matter how he was dressed, his techniques were impeccable.

Not everyone wanted to see him, however. When some people from the UK heard the news that he was the replacement, some immediately returned home. I, on the other hand, was intrigued to see what this mysterious master had to offer.

I had already heard whispers about how serious he was. For decades, when challengers came to Japan to test the effectiveness of *Ninpo taijutsu* (unarmed defense), Tanemura Sensei was usually the one who put them in their proper place. I was not about to miss the opportunity to see for myself.

BOJUTSU

We were in the camp's multipurpose room. It had a stage, a fireplace and a large open training area. Tanemura Sensei stayed on the floor level with the rest of us, and someone handed him a *rokushaku-bo* (six-foot staff). Nothing was pre-arranged. Within seconds the grandmaster was spinning the six-foot cudgel knowingly around and above his body. Even without a training partner, each movement clearly had a purpose. His posture and way of generating energy were unlike anything I had ever seen. It was fluid, but not like Kung Fu movie. It was powerful, but different than Okinawan karate-do.

The year before at the same camp another teacher had dazzled me. The problem was that I couldn't remember most of what I had seen. Anytime a student asked him to repeat a technique, he would simply change it and show a different (usually more complicated) variation. He told us to "play" with the moves and that "formlessness" was the highest form.

Tanemura Sensei was not that way. After a brief warm up, he started at the beginning. He taught us how to bow correctly with the staff. His attention to detail really changed the way I thought about the movements. Instantly, even the smallest gesture had profound meaning. He went on to explain that "the basics equal the highest techniques," and then he proved it.

When the swordsman who faced Soke finished the kneeling salutation, the Grandmaster rose with him in unison from the floor. Before both could even get to their feet and to the astonishment of everybody watching, Tanemura Sensei deftly launched a surprise strike. In a flash the opponent was beaten!

On purpose, Sensei had projected the extending staff mere inches from his opponent's head and toes. His opponent was stunned and helplessly checkmated. So, the victory was plain to see for everyone. "Even just your bowing can stop an attacker," the Grandmaster said with a smile.

TAIJUTSU

Sensei went on to show us the beginning techniques from the two other essential sections of all martial arts training: *taijutsu* (unarmed defense) and *biken-jutsu* (secret sword art). If a participant became confused, Tanemura Sensei did his utmost to guide the student's understanding. Alone or with the help of his black belt level students, Sensei led the class in scores of repetitions. He drilled us on the *kihon waza* (fundamental techniques). *Soke* (the Grandmaster) asked each of us to dig deep and "renshu," a statement which means to polish your techniques until they shine like a mirror.

While Tanemura Sensei demonstrated two hundred repetitions of ten different sets of *ninpo* push-ups, I thought to myself, "Now **this** is the kind of teacher I would like to train under." Even now, I have still retained much of what was taught that day.

The *taijutsu* training was a multifaceted event. In addition to daily sessions on grass as well as *tatami* mats, we covered *ukemi* (break-falls and rolls), *taisabaki* (evasion and body movement), *daken-taijutsu* (punching and kicking) and *jujutsu* (grappling art).

Tanemura Sensei also showed everyone some amazing videos from Japan. I'll never forget the first images from the *Honbu* (Headquarters) *Dojo* in Saitama prefecture.

The scenes in the video were surprising and inspiring. One clip featured students preparing to take turns facing the camera. They were waiting to be attacked in an oddly relaxed manner. Tanemura Sensei, himself, stood behind each candidate holding a *shinai* (bamboo sword). For a moment, everything was calm. But without visible warning, the scene erupted!

One by one, they would be stabbed from behind. But instead of being impaled, the respective students instinctively flew sideways, like a door opening. The point of the sword missed its mark and dramatically darted toward the video recorder lens. I had never imagined that martial arts training could be like this.

BIKENJUTSU

Bikenjutsu, or simply *kenjutsu* (sword art) as I knew it then, seemed a little more familiar. I had trained a little in *kendo* (modern fencing) and *iaido* (modern sword drawing). So, I thought that I had a handle on the use of the *katana* (Japanese sword). But, after being painfully corrected and relentlessly drilled on the basic cuts, my teenage mind was blown. Tanemura Sensei then started to lecture and introduced a secret sword skill totally foreign to me.

"If you can completely block your opponent's sword, you've already won. By blocking, I don't mean the kind of bashing of blades one sometimes sees in the ninja movies. Rather, I'm referring to the type of control that comes from more than the knowledge of technique. It is forged by keeping the proper heart/mind."

"Here is another master-level point of biken-jutsu; it is the rare ability for a swordsman to subdue his opponent without actually having to kill him…"

After that statement, Sensei set aside the basics and jumped to the master level. He ordered one of his highest ranked students to cut seriously with a *katana*. The grandmaster too was armed with a sword. And suddenly, there were two flashes of metal.

Using the dull side of the blade, the Grandmaster defended, deflecting the attack and executing a painful elbow lock in two swift motions. Following the breathtaking demonstration Tanemura Sensei added again, "The best swordsman wins without having to wound his adversary."

"Hajime mashite!" (Nice to meet you!) the Grandmaster said as we bowed, and he offered his hand. It was after class one evening when Tanemura Sensei had a bit of free time. Most of the camp participants had already left the training hall and spread out around the grounds. Only about ten people were in the room with us when I started my almost endless round of rapid-fire questions.

Sensei was flanked by Mr. Roy Ron from Israel. Ron *Shihan* is a master now but was more of a beginning black belt back then. Even though the Grandmaster spoke English very well, Ron *Shihan* was still helpful in translating my queries.

I was only nineteen years old, and I think that my age helped to soften Tanemura Sensei's view of my impatience and inquisitiveness. I asked lots of things that I shouldn't have about subjects that were way over my head. Sensei simply smiled through it all without getting too offended.

Finally, I asked permission to join his school. He eventually agreed. And at that moment, I truly stepped on the path to understanding and entering *Bumon* (the martial arts gate) and *Shumon* (the spiritual gate).

GRANDMASTER TANEMURA BIOGRAPHY
(Please see Chapter Notes section i)

Tanemura Tsunehisa was born on August 28th, 1947 in Saitama, Japan. As is the custom in several *Koryu* (ancient schools of Japanese *Budo*), he has also earned many martial art names including *Bi Koku Ryu* (mysterious black dragon) and *Fudo Masachika* (immovable righteous man). In addition, after being awarded the title of *Soke* (head master) of several family traditions, he symbolized his complete dedication by changing his given name to *Shoto* (Expertise of the Sword).

The Tanemura Family is of noble heritage tracing its lineage back to a son of the 59th Emperor of Japan. The family's ancestry came from the Sasaki Clan, which at one time ruled several *Ken* (prefectures). Relations of Takeda Shingen (the very famous *daimyo* of Yamanashi) intermarried with the Sasaki line.

Around the end of the Kamakura period (1195 AD) the clan took usage of the name Tanemura. Eventually, the household moved from Shiga-ken to Saitama-ken, in about 1570 AD controlling a hereditary fief there until the end of World War II.

.At the age of nine, Grandmaster Tanemura had already been initiated into the practice of *jujutsu* and the *kenjutsu* of Onoha Itoh Ryu and Shindo Munen Ryu. His father was an eighteenth-generation lord and martial art master in his own right. Therefore, it was not difficult for Tanemura Sensei to find his first teacher. Even so, the arduous and unrelenting training Soke had to endure was not for the weak-hearted.

The elder Tanemura was a very stern and strict teacher. Many times, the father would strongly strike his son with his fists, feet or wooden swords, rendering the primary school boy unconscious. *Kappo* (the ancient art of resuscitation) was frequently needed during training sessions. But in most cases, a simple bucket of cold water was sufficient.

As Tanemura Sensei grew in experience, he understood that martial arts were to be a very important force in his life. This realization fortified him. – In time, he mastered *taijutsu* (unarmed defense including strikes and blocks). He did so by vowing to train every day, no matter the conditions. Even when he was bed ridden, the young boy would sneak out and find a way to practice.

This determination and perseverance forged an unshakable spirit (*fudoshin*) and continues to guide the way the Grandmaster instructs his students.

SENSEI IN THE REAL WORLD

In 1971, Grandmaster Tanemura graduated with a degree in Law from Hosei University in Tokyo. In that same year, he entered the Tokyo Metropolitan Police Department. For over fourteen years Lieutenant Tanemura distinguished himself. On numerous occasions he used his *ninpo* and traditional *jujutsu* experience to subdue criminals, including members of the *yakuza* (Japanese Mafia).

In one instance, Tanemura Sensei single-handedly saved a police chief from an angry crowd of over fifty people armed with sticks and knives. In my years of training with Soke, I've heard many, many true-life examples such as this. The grandmaster sums it up simply, "I cannot count how many times I've used this martial art in real life situations!"

Because of his work as a detective, the grandmaster is always adept at imparting the practical side of the training, without sacrificing the dignity of the art's heritage.

THE FIRST NINPO MASTER TO VISIT THE WEST

In 1976, Tanemura Sensei became the first master from his tradition to be invited to show the true martial arts of *Ninpo* in the United States. Unfortunately, not everyone who attended this unique foreign seminar was ready to be a loyal student. They were also not wholly interested in the self-defense aspects of his art. In short, they wanted to test everything they saw.

Tanemura Sensei was violently challenged by seven different martial artists from various styles. Even though Soke was slightly disappointed by their conduct, the Grandmaster escaped unscathed. Tanemura Sensei also demonstrated in front of the Atlanta Metropolitan Police Department. They were so impressed they made him an honorary officer.

About a decade later, Grandmaster Tanemura was again invited to the US. This time he was more warmly received. I had the honor of being in attendance for this second visit. I've studied martial arts since early childhood, but nothing I have seen then or since has so completely inspired my practice and growth as much as Ninpo. Beyond all doubt, I know that this is what I need to study for my entire life.

QUALITY OF THE SPIRIT

Whenever I start teaching Ninpo to someone, I always try to check the quality of the person's spirit first. Is it good or bad, light or heavy? After this evaluation, I decide whether this person will be a worthy student or not. This is a Genbukan Dojo rule.

People's minds are continually changing. So, it can be challenging for them to maintain the same level of focus for an extended period of time. For these reasons, even after applicants have entered my school, their hearts unfortunately change for the worse.

For me, it is easy to see such changes. But, an interesting phenomenon also manifests during such times. A student, whose heart has changed, leaves of his own accord without a single word from me. For this person, the feeling of an honest dojo makes them leave. Ours is a Shinshin Shingan (spiritual heart/ mind, spiritual eyes) dojo, which is synonymous with honesty and purity.

If an enemy attacks with a weapon, students of this type of dojo can defend themselves without resorting to the same level of violence. At the highest level, they can utilize spiritual power alone. Of course, only a person whose heart reflects Shinshin Shingan is able to accomplish this. For this reason, we seek to understand the strategies of defense of the body, as well as the truth that is inherent in all religions.

By using this philosophy, a true ninja can develop spiritually and never lose energy by wandering from the middle way. He can also exemplify the law of both God and the martial artist; never kill anything except as a last resort – known as Shin Bujin Fuisatsu no Ho.

-Tanemura Shoto Sensei

AMATSU TATARA SPIRITUAL TEACHINGS

The most important points to understand about the Amatsu Tatara *Shumon* (spiritual teachings) are that BOTH regular training in the martial arts and properly conducting one's daily life are the mainstays of the teachings. Many priests, upon learning about Tanemura Sensei's spiritual background, have come to his home seeking to receive the highest-level transmissions of their own traditions.

After receiving these guests, the Grandmaster usually smiles and invites them to begin training by doing one of our most basic techniques, the *zenpo kaiten* (forward roll). Invariably, the bewildered aspirants always give Soke a confused look. They are quick to restate that they are holy men and not interested in studying *kobudo* (ancient martial arts). To this, Sensei answers the same way every time...

"Martial arts deeply teach the virtues necessary to understand the highest spiritual teachings without words. Through *Budo* you can truly know what it is to give up the ego." – Upon hearing this, most of the priests simply scratch their heads and run away.

AMATSU TATARA MARTIAL ARTS

To help students visualize the importance of each of the arts he teaches, Tanemura Sensei devised a simple representation: the spine is *Ninpo taijutsu*; the right arm is *biken-jutsu*; the left arm is *bojutsu*; the right leg is *jujutsu*; the left leg *Chugoku Kenpo* (Chinese martial arts); and finally, the heart is Amatsu Tatara *Shumon* (natural spiritual way).

JUJUTSU PHYSICAL TRAINING

Along with the *kyu* levels (progressive techniques taught before black belt), the first *ryu-ha kata* (classical school technique patterns) we learn in the *Kokusai Jujutsu Renmei* (International Jujutsu Federation) are from the *Hontai Takagi Yoshin Ryu*. The requirements are arranged so that at the end of each grade only one or two patterns need be memorized. This allows the student months to fully absorb the basic version of the *koshiki gata* (ancient forms).

Eventually over 100 kyu techniques are mastered. This includes over a dozen chosen specifically from the *Hontai Takagi Yoshin Ryu* scrolls. Only after the *shodan* (first-degree black belt) level does Tanemura Sensei begin to teach a multitude of *henka* (advanced variations).

Each of the *koshiki gata* is loaded with indispensable information. *Taisabaki* (proper body movement), classical self-defense and *zanshin* (awareness) are all drilled in detail. They are so important I've heard the grandmaster say many times, "If you don't understand these *kihon* (fundamentals), you don't know anything about traditional *jujutsu*."

AN ASAYAMA ICHIDEN RYU JUJUTSU TECHNIQUE

NINPO PHYSICAL TRAINING

The Genbukan *Ninpo Bugei* (martial arts) has a similar structure. There are also ten *kyu* levels, but more than double the techniques. Before *shodan* (first-degree black belt) the beginning student must learn almost 300 *taijutsu waza* (unarmed techniques). Only after these are mastered can they be ready to internalize the more spiritual aspects of the arts.

Even at white belt level, one of the first things discussed is one of the "*sanpo hiden*" (three secret methods of energy cultivation). The trinity of Heaven, Earth and Man is taught immediately in the first section. *Gassho* (hands in prayer position) representing the three are introduced as *rei* (bows). As training partners, we agree to assist each other's personal growth. Tanemura Sensei teaches that this maturity can only occur after overcoming life's obstacles, and no one is immune to this condition. We all have to work hard to advance to the next level.

As martial artists we have chosen to fight this battle eloquently in the dojo. We bring these challenges out in the open, so that we can physically and mentally deal with them on the mat. Count yourself lucky when you find a master who is wise enough to guide you to self-discovery and self-realization. But it is ultimately the student's responsibility to recognize that wisdom.

Tanemura Sensei says, "In daily life we must try to strike a balance: one-third work, one-third free time and one-third rest." How many of us can boast living such an orderly life? Over time, Amatsu Tatara martial artists learn to move towards balancing the scales. The *sanpo hiden* mentioned above is another way to organize our techniques and our minds.

KORYU KARATE PHYSICAL TRAINING

Among all the schools of *jujutsu* and *taijutsu*, the *Kijin Chosui Ryu* – also related to the famous *Kukishin Ryu* – focuses on techniques which bring certain victory. There are very few people who have mastered this *ryu-ha*, because traditionally only one person was allowed to inherit the true spirit and skills. This is the *daken-taijutsu* (striking and punching art) *kaiden* (master level) method, as described in the initiation instructions contained in the Amatsu Tatara *Tora no Maki* (Tiger Scroll).

Grandmaster Tanemura learned directly from Kobayashi Masao Sensei, Kimura Sensei and other grandmaster-level students of Takamatsu Sensei. Training in these traditional martial arts for over 60 years, Tanemura Sensei received the highest "Dragon" and "Tiger" scrolls from this most ancient and unbroken line of grandmasters.

Creating a systematic structure and teaching this devastating art to the public was a long-term goal of Takamatsu Sensei – one which he would not live long enough to fulfill. After decades of preparing to bring true *Kobudo* to the public, Grandmaster Tanemura has decided that it is finally time to complete Takamatsu Sensei's mission and share this once-secret art.

Tanemura Soke refers to this art as *Koryu* (classical or "old school") *Karate* (literally "China hand", not the "empty hand" as in Okinawan *Karate-do*) and what he teaches comes from the techniques of Kijin Chosui Ryu *daken-taijutsu* (striking hand technique) and Tenshin Ryu *koryu kenpo* (fist method).

Grandmaster Tanemura has developed a step-by-step system of *Kyu* levels and *Dan* levels (degrees of black belt) to help students absorb these advanced techniques.

A KYORYU KARATE TECHNIQUE

CONTINUED ON NEXT PAGE

HISTORY BECOMES THE PRESENT

Who was the link to the past? – How did these ancient traditions and secrets survive and continue into the twenty-first century? One man, Takamatsu Toshitsugu, was responsible for bridging the gap. He overcame many personal obstacles as well as the confusion brought on by a totally transformed homeland (for example, the turmoil after World War II), and successfully kept the most ancient

Japanese spiritual and martial art system alive. There are many stories to come about how fate brought together two masters and kept the flame from dying out.

TAKAMATSU TOSHITSUGU SENSEI

From the first day I heard about Takamatsu Sensei, I was in awe. The stories I listened to bordered on the supernatural. But as I got older, I wanted to know about the true person, not just the legend.

Some years ago, my teacher, Tanemura Sensei, published a newsletter that included some interesting information. For the first time, he released very personal documents related to Takamatsu Sensei. More than anything I had seen before, they painted a picture of a real man, complete with doubts, fears and fallibility.

Like anyone, he didn't start out as an accomplished master. Takamatsu Sensei began humbly and was tempered by many painful life experiences. But lucky for us, he eventually grew into his destiny to become one of the greatest martial artists ever born.

TAKAMATSU AS A CHILD

"As a child, I was a crybaby and a weakling, and I was not satisfied about it. During the dark of autumn under a willow tree, I watched other children playing Sumo. I became very sad as I thought about my situation. I wondered why I could not be more like the other kids. At this time I was only playing with girls. I was so depressed, and I thought that there was no cure for me. Many times I had such thoughts.

One day at school, all the members of our third grade class were assembled. There were about 100 of us. Sensei ordered that everyone must participate in a Sumo event. At this announcement I stood there shivering. This was my first experience. I started crying.

At school the Sensei's word was law, so I could not refuse to participate. I was seen weeping by some of the other children, who yelled, 'Sensei, this boy is crying!' Others taunted me, saying, 'You crybaby!' I became sadder. A watching teacher told me, 'Takamatsu, don't cry. Why cry at all?' At this, more tears came.

Then the head teacher called my name. It was my turn. I suddenly felt like a large rock had fallen on my head. In shock, I sort of stumbled up onto the platform to enter the Sumo ring. My opponent-to-be saw my condition and teased me about it. He pushed me around, but I did not go out of the ring. He came at me again, but I was so tired that I only turned aside a bit. He had come at me so strongly; he couldn't help but to run out of the ring. I was suddenly amazed to hear the teacher shout out, 'Takamatsu is the winner!'

Then the next boy to challenge me took hold of my neck and legs to try and put me down. I felt very horrified at this. So I refused to move. He fell down. Again, I had won. Everyone was cheering for me, the weakling. I could not understand this at all.

Then, the strongest of all my classmates came into the ring. He was very tall for his age and big-muscled like a real Sumo. He ran at me quickly, and not knowing what to do, I threw my arms up in front of me. The boy crashed into my block and fell back! – Thirteen more big guys were matched against me, but inexplicably, I still won. All of the people were shouting, 'Takamatsu is the strongest!'"

- Takamatsu Toshitsugu Sensei

TANEMURA'S SEARCH FOR MEANING PART I

I was born just after World War II. My mother and father were of noble lineage and, at one time, very rich. Our family owned most of the town where I grew up and enjoyed an exceptionally good life. I was the youngest child and born after most of the wealth was gone. So, my early experiences were a bit different than those of my older, more privileged siblings.

After Japan lost the war, most everything was taken away. With only a small percentage of their former holdings, my parents had trouble even putting food on the table. On top of this, a terrible hurricane came that year. It flooded our house and water rose to the ceiling. Growing crops became impossible. The whole country seemed to be starving.

Now that I am older, I understand that these conditions were actually very good for me. Hardship and hunger taught me patience. Suffering and striving taught me to never give up. My mother said that Fudo Myo-oh (the unshakable angel of righteousness) must have been my guardian spirit.

-Tanemura Shoto Sensei

FUDOSHIN - INDOMITABLE SPIRIT

Takamatsu Sensei once said, "The heart supports us in the ups and downs of life. To have an indomitable spirit means getting up after every fall. No one can reach his or her goal without this spirit. A ninja needs an exceptionally strong heart, like grass that is stepped on many times but never gives up living. It is from this notion that the ninja were once called kusa (grass)."

An unskillful student when compared to the others, I practiced harder than they did. The greater the injury, the more I exerted myself. This is what training truly means! Through my trials, I have developed and continue to do my best with this same spirit. Of course, there have been times when I wanted to stop marital arts altogether. I went through many mental hardships, and my experience has convinced me that the Amatsu Tatara way is the only path for me.

My purpose in life is to find the truth following this way. My mission is to teach and show people the blossom of virtue that can be discovered. With strong conviction, I will strive for both my students and for myself.

A martial art is different from a sport. In a real fight, your opponent will not show any mercy toward you for your disabilities. It is a mistake to be discouraged by a few broken bones. Remember this during regular training; otherwise the strong spirit required for physical and mental self-defense will not be there when you need it most.

- Tanemura Shoto Sensei

HANBOJUTSU AGAINST A SLASH
WITH A SHORT SWORD

GIKAN RYU KOPPO – JUTSU SECRET HISTORY

The tenth generation *soke* (grandmaster) of Gikan Ryu *koppo-jutsu*, Uryu Gikanbo went by the same name as the first. He was a very experienced warrior. During the famous rebellion of "Tenchu Gumi no Ran" at the end of Edo period, he fought bravely. On August 17th, 1863, after enjoying tremendous success in the battle, he was injured by a rifle shot to the shoulder. Even though he was wounded and bleeding, he continued defending with his one, good arm.

Fighting to the point of exhaustion and suffering many sword cuts, he retired from the melee behind a temple. On his way to join the battle, Iga warrior, Ishitani Matsutaro Takakage, discovered him. Ishitani took Gikanbo back to his own home to recover. Later, Ishitani was repaid for this kindness as grandmaster Uryu taught him the Gikan Ryu techniques. Ishitani Matsutaro was already a master of the highest grade in several schools including Hontai Takagi Yoshin Ryu and Kukishin Ryu.

Gikan Ryu is almost totally unknown to the public and the secret techniques were handed down only to the next generation head master. The founder, Uryu Hogan Gikanbo, lived during the Eiroku Era (1558 - 1570). He was a ruler of Kawachi no Kuni (near the modern city of Osaka) with a clan castle called Uryu-jo. He was a true warrior and marital artist. His original intentions were to maintain permanent peace in the country. From his teachings there comes a slogan: "*bufu ni sente nashi*" (from this side the first strike will not come).

The Gikan Ryu was greatly influenced by a Chinese style taught by Cho Gyoko (a female martial artist). Gikanbo merged the system with native Japanese martial arts. The aggregate style contains unique kicks, punches and throws. There is even a special fist strike that can break a sword.

In ancient times, the term "jujutsu" was not used. The styles were referred to as *kosshi-jutsu* (muscle and nerve attacks), *koppo-jutsu* (skeletal and weak point attacks), and *daken-taijutsu*.

In Meiji Era, Ishitani was given employment by the father of Takamatsu Sensei at the family match factory. It was during this time that Ishitani started to teach Takamatsu Sensei. As Ishitani's successor, Takamatsu Sensei was granted the grandmastership of the next generation title in Hontai Takagi Yoshin Ryu, Kukishin Ryu, and Gikan Ryu, among other family traditions. In the first month of 1963, 100 years after Ishitani Sensei met Gikanbo, Sato Kinbei Sensei was awarded headmastership in Gikan Ryu *koppo-jutsu*.

Until Tanemura Sensei was taught the school, any information concerning Gikan Ryu has been held exclusively by Sato Sensei. In all the various forms of *kuden* (oral secrets), *makimono* (scrolls) and *densho* (secret texts), the knowledge was his alone. In 1989, Tanemura Shoto Sensei was chosen to succeed him as the fourteenth grandmaster.

A single person can have a profound effect on the continuity of generations of accumulated knowledge and experience. Though it is a very important school, Gikan Ryu is only one of the family branches that have grown out of the *honbu* (the trunk of the tree). To understand more completely, we must look back further and deeper; back to the beginning and the root of our teachings, the Amatsu Tatara scrolls (please see Chapter III for more information).

SHODAN TESTING

Testing and ranking has always been a subject of some controversy in every martial arts tradition. Each teacher, it seems, has inherited their own special method of guaranteeing that the tradition continues the "true" way.

There are three basic types of tests in the Amatsu Tatara arts, tests for the *Kyu*, *Dan*, and master levels. – *Kyu* level techniques are concerned primarily with physical and kinesthetic ability. In the old days, there was little need for standardized *Kyu* level test progression. Classes were very small. Frequently most, or all, of the practitioners were blood-related. And, the *Shihan* (master) knew intimately the strengths and weaknesses of his *deshi* (disciple). The basics could be taught, and the emphasis could be shifted without having to rely on a detailed syllabus.

In the late 1800's, Dr. Jigoro Kano (the founder of Judo and a good friend of Takamatsu Sensei) blazed the trail and established a universal *kyu-dan* grading system that is still followed today. However, not until the mid-twentieth century did the Amatsu Tatara arts adopt a similar system.

Our ancient, more personal way of teaching was generally available only to relatives. Of course, that method uniquely addressed each student's weaknesses. However, this intimate style is almost impossible to implement on a large scale. These days, literally thousands of students need to be able to demonstrate the same patterns, often without the benefit of actually meeting the grand master. Therefore, Tanemura Sensei had to establish a universal method and common standard for all the students around the world.

I was honored to be part of the Genbukan as some of these standards were being created. Even so, it would take me decades of teaching this curriculum to fully understand the depth of genius that was imparted by my teacher.

MY BLACK BELT IS TAKEN AWAY

In the second year after meeting Tanemura Sensei, I flew to New York City. Soke was eager to see what I had actually remembered from a collection of seminars and a few private lessons. The new *Kyu* level system was just being implemented and many of the American black belt students were unfamiliar with the exact structure. Therefore, the grandmaster personally check-tested me on each aspect of the pre-*shodan* techniques.

I encountered some difficulty training with the grandmaster at first. His English was limited and my Japanese at that time was non-existent. – It was very difficult to understand what was happening. Everything I did seemed wrong, and at each turn I was afraid he might get frustrated and give up on me.

Over the next five days and with the help of Okayasu *Shihan* and the late Nagamoto *Shihan* (the Grandmaster's two highest level students in the world), Tanemura Sensei remolded and pieced together my techniques. With aching joints and limbs, I received my *san kyu* grade (a high green belt level). The level was high enough that I could maintain my status as a group leader, but the black belt that I received from another teacher would have to be put into storage. At that time, I was the lowest level instructor in the United States.

THE AUTHOR WITH OKAYASU SHIHAN, THE HIGHEST LEVEL DISCIPLE OF THE SOKE

In 1989, Tanemura Sensei came to Milwaukee for the first time. On the flight to Wisconsin he had a strange experience. When I met him at the airport he looked like he had been crying. At that time, we were not very close, so he didn't completely explain what had happened. (See Chapter Notes Section ii)

MY TEST AND SPIRITUAL INTIATION

After establishing his hotel room, my black belt test was the first order of business. After my experience in New York, I was better prepared and Tanemura Sensei was pleased with my performance. He did several things that I had never seen before. Immediately after receiving my license, Tanemura Sensei ordered me to close my eyes in meditation. He touched my forehead and gauged my level of concentration. When my mind was ready, he said some special words and wrote an ancient glyph. Then he presented me with a flat scroll. The Grandmaster explained that it was too powerful for me to display openly at my low level of development. It would be a full 28 years before I found out its full meaning.

Tanemura Sensei was also impressed by a question I had asked. Again, there was a reference to the idea of *sanpo hiden* (three secret methods). *Tenryaku Uchu Gassho*, *Futen Goshin Gassho*, and *Hanno Bonitsu Gassho* are the names of the three hand positions taught at white belt. Tanemura Sensei remarked that very few students had ever bothered to ask him about the seemingly unimportant first level, and he shared several *kuden* about these hand gestures. The next day, he produced for me the hand-written *futen* characters and named my dojo the *Futen Dojo*.

DEVELOPMENT OF FUTEN SHIBU
PART ONE

By 1989, my *Futen Dojo* had fewer than twenty regular students. I was very poor and had trouble making rent every month. I had survived for two years, because of the charity of a friend who owned a martial arts school. He allowed me to "rent" his space several days a week, but most months he just simply "forgot" to collect the twenty percent that he was supposed to receive.

At the 1990 *Taikai* (International Conference) in New York, I was still very skinny. Though I didn't eat much, I couldn't afford to dine at any of the big city restaurants. To tell the truth, I actually brought food with me and used the air conditioner in my hotel room to keep it from spoiling. That Saturday evening, there was a lavish *Taikai* banquet. Of course, it was too rich for my budget and I couldn't attend. But from outside, it sounded like everybody was having fun.

After everyone had enjoyed the food and entertainment, I straggled in to say good night to the senior teachers. It was very hot that day, and even after sundown the humidity was stifling. Choosing comfort over what was appropriate, I was wearing a light-colored rayon shirt with buttons, khaki shorts and rubber-soled dock shoes.

When I walked in, I immediately noticed that Tanemura Sensei seemed to be disappointed with me. Around the same moment, I realized that all the people at the head table were wearing suits or other evening attire. I was seriously under-dressed. – Later the Grandmaster explained that in a "ceremony party" one never walks in wearing "hot pants." He felt embarrassed for me even though I obviously didn't understand the dress code.

Eventually, I had to do something about my serious lack of funding. I decided to write a few articles for a small martial arts magazine. I guess that the strategy worked, because before long I was receiving offers to teach seminars all across the United States.

Over the next few years, I was invited to teach in many US states including: Illinois, Ohio, Washington, Colorado, Utah, Texas, New York, Alabama, Connecticut, Florida, California and Georgia. And, these international magazine articles were seen by interested instructors from all over the world. Since then, I've helped to personally introduce the Genbukan arts to students in several other countries including: Canada, Spain, Italy, Brazil, Argentina, and Chile.

NIDAN

弐

段

"An army can be likened to water, for just as flowing water avoids the heights and hastens to the lowlands, so an army avoids strength and strikes weakness."
-Sun Tzu

CHAPTER II

SENSEI SAVES A WOMAN IN AIRPORT

Grandmaster Tanemura and I were on an escalator going down at Milwaukee's international airport. Tanemura Sensei seemed to notice that something dangerous was about to happen. An older woman, probably in her 70s, had stepped onto the upward-moving escalator. She was awkwardly holding a bag that seemed much too heavy for her to handle. As the metal stairs rose higher and higher, her grip on the uneven suitcase became less and less secure. Unfortunately, she continued to hold tight even when the weight started to pull her off-balance.

Before I could react, Sensei had already vaulted over the railing. Her stairs kept moving skyward, so he didn't have enough time to prevent the old woman from falling. The back of her head struck the jagged steps very hard, and the crimson blood contrasted sharply with her completely white hair.

Tanemura Sensei was the only one around to help her to her feet. By the time I managed to join them on the top landing, the grandmaster had already used two pressure points on the back of her neck to slow the bleeding. He had also borrowed a towel from a server at a restaurant and was trying to comfort her as best he could.

As busy travelers continued coming up from the check-in desk, the slow-motion quality of the escalator added a surreal feeling to the whole incident. Seeing the surprised look on people's faces as they realized what had happened was strange. Their smiles and excitement quickly turned to concern and worry. But, the woman's reaction to Tanemura Sensei and me was even more unnerving.

This elderly lady didn't at all appreciate an Asian man touching her for any reason. She did not see him as a savior; rather her strong prejudice had not at all been dulled by her disorientation. In addition, my dark face was also an unwelcome sight, which made me feel all the more uncomfortable.

I shook it off and alerted the paramedics. They responded quickly to the situation. After they had stabilized the woman, they complimented Sensei on his administration of first aid. The lady, on the other hand, offered no words of thanks. Even so, Sensei was satisfied and happy because she was safe.

In all the excitement we had almost forgotten that Sensei had a plane to catch. We had to sprint to the gate, but before he boarded the plane Tanemura Sensei said to me, "Perhaps saving people's lives is part of our mission also."

THE INTENTION OF NINPO

Martial arts contribute to society in that their original intention is the protection of country, family and oneself. There were many who changed this because they believed that the sword was only a tool to cut people down.

Within the martial arts world there are also the sayings: "Do not deliver the first blow; keep the sword in the scabbard; and win without loss of blood."

Though we can hear these principles from almost all the masters, the ninja were and are the only ones taking them to heart.

- Takamatsu Toshitsugu Sensei

BUTOKU – MARTIAL ARTS VIRTUES

According to one Japanese dictionary, butoku means to make one better by behaving with upright conduct or to have high morality. In my opinion one should have many qualities including:

仁 **Jin - benevolence or compassion**

義 **Gi - courageousness**

礼 **Rei - etiquette or manners**

智 **Chi - wisdom**

忠 **Chu - loyalty**

孝 **Ko - obedience**

真 **Shin - truthfulness**

美 **Bi -gracefulness**

善 **Zen - goodness and kindness**

It is fundamental to develop these qualities, but it is using them that is of utmost importance. All my pupils should have justice, righteousness and goodness within them. There will, of course, be times when it'll be difficult to judge what is good and what is bad. However, there is a saying that goes, "If one sees an injustice and does not intervene, this is a worse injustice."

—Tanemura Shoto Sensei

TAKAMATSU SENSEI'S HISTORY IN BRIEF

Takamatsu Sensei was born in Meiji 22 (1889), on March 10th, in the town of Akashi in Hyogo Prefecture. His parents were Takamatsu Gishin (father) and Takamatsu Fushi (mother). – The Takamatsu family originated in Ise at Matsugashima, where the family was daimyo of Hosokubi Castle. An important ancestor was daimyo Takamatsu Masatoshi connected with the famed Atsuta Shrine, where Fujiwara Toshihiro presented him with the Amatsu Tatara scroll.

Takamatsu Sensei's father received the degree of Dai-Ajari (spiritual master) from a mountain priest named Kumano Shugendo. His father was also a company president in Akashi and a special committee member of the prefecture government. With the Amatsu Tatara scroll, Gishin had very deep connections to the Kuki family. Takamatsu Sensei helped the Kuki family to update the scroll by copying it in ornate script and providing explanations where needed.

At nine years old, Takamatsu Sensei went to Arate-cho, to study under the guidance of his mother's grandfather, Toda Shinryuken Masamitsu. He was instructed in several schools of Kobudo (ancient martial arts) including Shinden Fudo Ryu, Togakure Ryu and Koto Ryu. He received the menkyo kaiden for each of these.

After Toda Sensei died in his 80's, in 1912, Takamatsu Sensei went back to Akashi. Under Mizuta Yoshitaro, he studied the

Fujita line of Takagi Yoshin Ryu until receiving his menkyo kaiden. At 17, under Ishitani Matsutaro, a relative who worked in the family match factory, he studied a different line of Takagi Yoshin Ryu, Gikan Ryu, Kukishin Ryu and Shinden Muso Ryu. Again he earned his menkyo kaiden in each ryu-ha. Four years later, Ishitani Sensei died with his head in Takamatsu Sensei's lap. He was sixty-four years old.

Takamatsu Sensei's long life he had many trials and adventures. Here are just a few of them:

- *Age 13: Takamatsu Sensei fights scores of hoodlums on the street and wins.*

- *Age 16: Wins a dojo challenger match against fighters of the Musashi Ryu.*

- *Age 19: Truly fights for his life for the first time.*

- *Age 21: For more than ten years experiences war in China, Mongolia, and Manchuria. In his diary he said that he had 12 duels to the death, and seven competition matches.*

- *Age 25: In China he helps found a Japanese Martial Arts Federation and fights matches to decide the leadership with six practitioners of Kodokan Judo and Kito Ryu Jujutsu. He wins becoming the director with a following of 3000 students. He continues to study and masters 18 forms of Chinese and Korean martial Arts.*

- *Age 33: Returns to Japan. He was called the Mongolian Tiger in China, yet in Japan he was called Yamato no Neko (Japanese Spirit Cat). From there he lived quietly (mostly) teaching others until he died.*

On the 2nd of April 1972, a great star rejoined the heavens.

-Tanemura Shoto Sensei

WHAT'S IN A NAME?

At birth, Takamatsu Sensei was given the name of Hisatsugu. But when he became an adult he changed it slightly. Keeping the same kanji (Chinese characters) and using a different reading, he took the name Toshitsugu.

Takamatsu Sensei's first martial arts name was Kikaku (demon horn). Later he gave this name to his pupil, Nobuyoshi Takeuchi. Afterward, Takamatsu Sensei took another name Chosui (pure water). But eventually he granted it to another student Takashi Ueno, who then became famous as Chosui Ueno.

Sato Kimbei Sensei was given the soke title from Takamatsu Sensei but didn't need a martial arts name, because he already had one, Jushinsai (lilac heart man). Sato Kimbei Sensei was senior to Ueno Takashi, and was responsible for introducing him to Takamatsu Sensei. Afterwards, Takamatsu Sensei took two other names that he used until his death and never passed on to anyone. One was Yokuoh (leaping and running in the sky old man), with the other being Garakutabujin (enjoy sketching martial artist).

-Tanemura Shoto Sensei

GRANDMASTER TANEMURA'S QUEST FOR MEANING II

THE WRONG QUESTIONS

"Father, why am I alive?"...

"Mother, what is my purpose on this earth?"...

To these questions my parents answered, "Be silent, Tsunehisa-kun. You are only five years old. You should be playing with toys, not having these kinds of thoughts."

But my heart was not satisfied. Between the ages of 5 and 8 years old, I interrogated aunts, uncles and grandparents; anyone who I thought was older and wiser. Yet, none of them could give me a straight answer. They all thought that I was strange and that I would get over it… But, I didn't.

- Tanemura Shoto Sensei

RESCUED AGAIN

"Help! Help! Save him!" a neighbor girl screamed. I couldn't hear her that well, because my head was already submerged. I had not found the answers for which I was searching, so I decided to end my meaningless life.

"Got you!" said the man who lived next to the river. This was not the first time that he had had to fish me out of the green water.

My mother was at her wit's end. Before the war, she had lived like a princess. Wealth had given her a sense of security and well-being. But by the time I was born, all of that peace and prosperity had been torn from her life.

To make matters worse, I was a problem child. I always asked senseless questions. Malnutrition made me small and weak, and though she did everything in her power to keep me alive, I repaid her kindness by becoming suicidal. At that time, I was about nine years old and something was about to change.

The head priest paused and said matter-of-factly, "Your son is very special. He has an important mission…." I couldn't understand everything they said, because I was so young. But soon after that, I started training in the martial arts.

-Tanemura Shoto Sensei

MOM AND DAD

My mother was a striving and steady, gentle personality. She was very kind and sincere to all those whom she met. Especially for the sake of her children she would sacrifice her own needs to see that theirs' were attended to. She was gentle and favoring towards me. She always believed in me and had mercy for my minor indiscretions.

Through the example of her life, she taught me to value the virtues of faith, mercy, and charity.

My father was a very strict teacher, from him I learned to persevere and never give up.

- Tanemura Shoto Sensei

SPIRITUAL CONCENTRATION

All martial arts have, as a goal, the development of spiritual concentration, Seishin-toitsu. In Ninpo this is the most fundamental teaching. The meaning of Seishin-toitsu is the ability to reach a state of naturalness through meditation. For the warrior, it is especially challenging to reach this state. Because, he places himself on the border between life and death and must take action. Yet, it is still our duty.

Only with great patience is spiritual concentration possible. – For the first third of this type of training, our efforts seem to yield no obvious return. For the second third, our dedication gives an equal measure of benefit. For the last third of one's training history, past efforts have accumulated merit and finally yield a wealth of understanding. The student receives seemingly miraculous returns on their heart-felt investments, without conscious effort.

-Tanemura Shoto Sensei

MEETING SATO KIMBEI SENSEI

SATO SENSEI AND TANEMURA SENSEI

In 1991, Dr. Kimbei Sato came to teach in the U.S. for the first time. He was one of Takamatsu Sensei's top students and received several grandmasterships by 1952. Among other arts, Sato Sensei was granted the *soke* title in Kukishin Ryu *bojutsu*, Hontai Takagi Yoshin Ryu *jujutsu*, and Gikan Ryu *koppo-jutsu* (Please see Chapter Notes section iii) from Takamatsu Sensei.

As a medical doctor during WWII, Sato Sensei worked in a military hospital in China. He was always fascinated by Chinese culture and martial arts. So, in his spare time he embarked on a quest to find the best traditional Kung Fu (Wushu) masters. Decades before Takamatsu Sensei had also lived in China, but the political and social situation was very different. As part of an occupying army, Sato Sensei's request to be a serious student was met with some skepticism. Yet eventually, his persistence paid off and he found the instruction he sought.

For the Chinese masters, discipline and dedication were absolute. To prove his sincerity, Dr. Sato had to start learning without the benefit of any verbal instruction. In the beginning, he was assigned only short sets of basic movements to repeat over and over. This went on for the first three years, and though he spoke Chinese fluently, he had little need for his language skills while training.

One of the things that truly fascinated Dr. Sato was the Chinese emphasis on the health benefits of martial arts. He quickly found out that learning the internal training (breathing, qigong and energy cultivation) was actually more difficult (and many times more expensive) than learning the external.

"For each of these postures, I paid a thousand dollars," said Sato Sensei to a group of about 50 black belts gathered for instructor training. Tanemura Sensei added later in private that between travels to China and hosting Kung Fu masters in Japan, Sato Sensei spent a great amount of money learning these arts.

THE EMPEROR'S QIGONG

Tanemura Sensei and Sato Sensei introduced us to *qigong* training (*kiko*, in Japanese, but another version is called *seiko*) by teaching a set of nine static postures. "*Qi*" (*ki* in Japanese) means internal energy, and "*gong*" refers to achievement or control gained over time.

There are hundreds of schools of thought when it comes to this type of internal training. However in my experience, this simple but sublime set of exercises, consistently gives the most benefit in the least amount of time. I also heard that at least one of the emperors of China, having access to every credible source, actually practiced these same exercises.

To begin with, it's proper form, consistency, and mental focus that matters more than how long the postures are held. Proper form summons the *ki*, consistency guarantees steady progress, and mental focus keeps the energy from dissipating.

At first, I couldn't believe how difficult it was to simply stand still with my arms over my head. But soon, *qi* started gathering in my lower abdomen and was eventually conducted to the middle of my palms. After that, my fingers opened slowly like flowers in sunlight, allowing my hands to float effortlessly from position to position. This feeling was a new sensation. *Qigong* added a spectacular dimension to my understanding of the potential of martial arts training.

THE DANGER OF MIXING MARTIAL ARTS

Tanemura Sensei was extremely fortunate to be able to master so many different martial arts family traditions to their highest levels. Many of these schools turned out to be related to each other in ways only understood by the Grandmasters. In my dictionary, this should not be defined as "mixing."

In contrast, I've also met many martial artists who were what I call, 'collectors of black belts.' They receive a little bit of training in one system, and then skip on to another style without ever delving into and discovering the deeper secrets of the first. I believe that a second-degree black belt in five systems does not equal a tenth degree in one system. – Of course, my teacher understands this very well, and I'm grateful that I follow his advice.

YAGYU SHINGAN RYU

The second thing that Sato Sensei introduced at the Taikai that really made a deep impression on me was the Yagyu Shingan *Ryu*. This was a true Japanese battlefield art, whose practitioners wore a full set of armor and screamed at each other at the top of their lungs. Sato Sensei's directions were translated and demonstrated by Grandmaster Tanemura. Some found the basic training monotonous, repeating the same sixteen movements endlessly. Even so, I found them inspiring and set out to master the system.

At first sight, I "stole" as many of the *kata* variations as I could (in the old days, even taking notes – in front of the master – was forbidden). It became easier over time, because the *kata* seemed to teach me to adapt perfectly when faced with more than a half-dozen different attacks. When Tanemura Sensei returned to my dojo, I showed him the pieces that I was able to reconstruct. Though my techniques were far from perfect, he seemed happy with my enthusiasm.

Because of my diligence, Sensei promised to train me in this ryu-ha. I came to find out, the highest levels of the system were not taught with words. In addition to thousands of solitary repetitions, I also received one on one instruction without the benefit of any dialogue. I was not allowed to ask questions and was painfully reminded when I made mistakes. After over five years of refinement, I received the first mastership scroll in Yagyu Shingan ryu. Twelve years later, I received another.

AMATSU TATARA SPIRITUAL TEACHINGS II

The Ninja Seishin poem is a traditional verse for guiding a ninja's heart. Recited at the beginning of each class by all Genbukan students, this verse acts as a key for connecting one's heart with that of Heaven.

"Ninja Seishin towa, shin-shin-shiki o shinobu, Ninniku Seishin o konpon tosuru. Chijoku o shinonde urami o hojisaru, nintai seishin o yashinau kotoni hajimaru monode aru. Nin towa, Kokoro no ueni yaiba o oite, yaiba de hito o kizutsuketari suruyona monodewa-naku, kajo

waraku, hana no gotoki joai o motte, Heiwa o tanoshimu monode aru. Yueni, tai o motte, Shizen ni aite no ken o sake, sugata o kesu, kyojitsu tenkan no myo-o-e, iccho kuni no tametoka, gi no tame ni, chi-sui-ka-fu-ku no Dai Shizen o riyo-shite, aite o taosu (seisuru) koto ga, ninja no konpon gensoku de aru."

Forbearance Spirit

The essence of the ninja spirit is fortitude. It is based on cultivating a forbearing spirit by training the body heart/mind and subconscious. Endure shame and let go of resentment. The origin is patience. "*Nin*" (endurance) is not placing the sword above the heart to injure others. It means "*Kajo Waraku*," feeling compassionate, pure and tender like a flower. Nin is the propagation of peace and enjoyment of life. Therefore your body will naturally avoid the opponent's sword avoid, and one's own form will attain the skill to make falsehood and unpreparedness transform and disappear. We use this truth in defense against enemies of justice, society and country. Using the nature's Earth, Water, Fire, Wind and Air (sky). The fundamental principle of the Ninja is thus.

KUKISHIN RYU BOJUTSU

九鬼神流棒術

A BASIC BOJUTSU AGAINST SWORD TECHNIQUE

NIDAN TESTING

I heard one time that if nothing difficult or challenging happens between your degrees of black belt, you have no business testing for the next level. In our tradition, Tanemura sensei decides when a person is ready for such an examination and, looking back, I personally haven't known my teacher to be wrong.

When I took my *nidan* test, the *ninpo* and *jujutsu* branches of our tradition were taught simultaneously. As I mentioned in Chapter I, the kyu levels included over 300 techniques. Each degree of black belt also contained techniques from about 5 separate family traditions and could number close to 100 waza. One of the ways to translate the word *Genbukan* is "infinite martial school." Indeed, the sheer depth and breadth of these traditions definitely make this statement true.

To prepare for the coming ordeal, I used my students as Guinea pigs. Sometimes I would introduce as many as 27 new techniques in one 3-hour class, before I established an after-hours training partner. Over time, it is hoped that the purpose of the dojo is more to aid the students than the teacher. But in truth, the teaching goes both ways.

Tanemura Sensei returned to Milwaukee every year. Ernest Wilhelm was my highest-level student at the time. I beat him up daily, so he was the perfect choice to be my *uke* (partner who received the *waza*). He suffered through hours of relentless strikes, throws and chokes, not only receiving the eighty-five *nidan taijutsu* techniques, but also scores of *hanbojutsu* (three foot stick art) and *jojutsu* (four foot stick art) *waza*. After a two-hour review of my form and spirit, the grandmaster promoted me to second-degree black belt, as well as granting me the first level masterships in short and medium staff fighting.

Never before had I been tested for such a long period of time. Rather than being exhausted by the experience, I felt inspired and invigorated. So much so, that I took up a challenge given to me years before in New York....

A HANBOJUTSU TECHNIQUE AGAINST A STAB WITH THE SHORT SWORD

TIME FOR SOME EXERCISE

Decades ago in New York City, Tanemura Sensei had challenged all of the instructors to do special types of push-ups. First, he did these exercises right along with us. Doing a hundred dip push-ups was just a warm up for the grandmaster. The other variations of the exercises were a little more complicated. Each set of ten was completed using a different hand form. Everything from wrists to fingertips was utilized, but the last two were the most difficult.

The first of those is called, *shikan-ken* (extended knuckle). It uses the middle finger's knuckle to support most of the body's weight. The rest of the fingers resemble a cat's paw and strengthen the hand position. The last push-up involved, called the *boshi-ken* (stick finger) hand form, supports one's weight exclusively on the tips of the thumbs.

On a *tatami* (mat) these ten sets are very difficult. But back then, Sensei's challenge had each *Genbukan* instructor trying it on a hard wood floor. At that time, I could do the first variation, but it wasn't until after I passed my *nidan* that my fingers were strong enough to do the *boshi-ken* style.

MY DUEL WITH SENSEI

On the way to Sensei's hotel room, I dropped down and executed a few one thumb push-ups for good measure. Tanemura sensei seemed amused, but once we entered his suite he asked me to demonstrate something a bit more frightening.

Clearing a space in the middle of the living room area, we faced off each holding a *shinai* (bamboo sword). We both held the weapons in *hasso no kamae* (eight-directions posture). I wasn't completely sure if this duel was part of the test or something just to keep my ego in check. Sensing my bewilderment, Tanemura sensei explained the rules.

"Hit me as fast as you can."

Without thinking, I launched a strike to the middle of Soke's forehead. Before my sword reached its mark, however, the grandmaster had already responded with an attack of his own. In less than a second, both of my wrists were stinging and my *shinai* lay on the floor.

"Pick it up," he commanded. So again, we faced off. This time I feigned a little forward, before striking with ever-greater ferocity. The second time was slightly different. I felt his sword on a single point of my left forearm, which stopped my attack but did not cause me to drop the bamboo. The pain was quickly becoming unbearable, so I humbly bowed and asked him to explain the lesson.

During the test, Tanemura Sensei had observed a "hitch" in my swing, an opening that compromised my staff and sword techniques. He expertly shared how to correct the error and I was deeply grateful.

THE DEVELOPMENT OF THE FUTEN SHIBU PART TWO

By 1990, the Genbukan Futen Dojo had moved to its own location. The building was an old, vacant community center west of the river (not the best side of town to be on at that time). Upstairs there was an abandoned movie theater and downstairs a dilapidated bowling alley. The good news was that there was a large amount of space available for not a lot of money. The bad news was that it was a "fixer-upper". Among many other improvements, I had to build a forty-foot wall to keep everything separate. This was only the beginning.

The ceiling was between twelve and fourteen feet high, and the sheets of wallboard came only in eight-foot sections. These gaps presented a problem when the bats that lived on the top floor decided to pay me a visit, while I was teaching class.

As the black rodents darted and swooped, I had to think fast. Underneath the mats were wide pieces of cardboard. We pulled them up quickly, and I instructed my students to open the door. Next, they were told to form two lines facing their partners. – One-by-one the bats found their way to the exit through the tunnel of cardboard. We finished the wall with plastic sheeting the next week, but our worst challenge was yet to come.

The winter that year was one of the coldest on record in the State of Wisconsin. Tanemura Sensei was coming back to Milwaukee for the second time, and my dojo didn't even have heat. Everyday I had to chip away ice in the toilet bowl with a wooden short sword. This continued until one day the temperature became so extreme that the whole unit cracked open completely!

My children's class was understandably small. Only two small boys braved the elements with sweaters and four pairs of socks under their uniforms. On the side of the main mat, I had an industrial strength kerosene heater that produced a flame that was over three feet long. Between techniques we removed our gloves and warmed our hands. My landlords had promised me a furnace months before, so I decided to stop paying rent until it was installed.

Finally, just days before the second Milwaukee seminar with Grandmaster Tanemura, the heating company truck came and we got relief from the bitter cold. Just in time.

SANDAN

三段

"Know your enemy and know yourself and in a
hundred battles you will never be in peril."
-Sun Tzu

CHAPTER III

MY FIRST TRIP TO JAPAN

FINDING THE HONBU DOJO

In the winter of 1992, my family drove me to the airport for my first trip to Japan. Just before we entered the on-ramp to the freeway, however, the car broke down. Luckily, I was able to reach a student by phone who worked at the downtown Hyatt Regency Hotel. He commandeered the hotel shuttle and got me to the airport just in time to make my flight. – After more than 16 hours of travel, I stepped onto the runway in Narita, Japan and took a bus to the terminal.

My first passenger train from Narita airport to the center of Tokyo was very comfortable. The Keisei Skyliner boarding platform was connected to the terminal. So, I could take the express directly into Ueno Station, the hub of all travel in Tokyo. The second leg of my journey was far more stressful and confusing.

In Ueno, I had to negotiate scores of different subway routes represented by a rainbow of colors. I'd never seen so many people in one place at one time in my life. Finally, I found the correct direction and color just in time to catch the rush hour train.

The metro cars were so over-packed with humans, white-gloved employees literally had to shove people's limbs in against the sliding doors for them to close. I stood betwixt a sea of commuters. My body helplessly swayed to the rhythm of the stopping and starting of the subway train. My duffle bag and suitcase had no permanent resting place, and several people politely endured being struck by my shifting luggage. After one more local train and a cab ride, I finally arrived across from the grandmaster's house.

In those days there were no streetlights near Sensei's rural home. As I walked from the main road, the surrounding rice fields and vegetable gardens were almost pitch black. Somewhere a dog was barking at an unseen enemy. The air was earthy, and unfamiliar smells came from the noodle shop and country road itself.

As I stood at the gateway, I felt a little nervous at first. But after composing myself and ringing the bell, the door slid open. I bowed and was accepted into the *Genbukan Honbu Dojo* (main headquarters' school).

MOVING INTO THE APARTMENT

When I arrived in the dojo, class was still in progress. Immediately following the late-night training session, Tanemura Sensei escorted me to the small apartment where I'd be living. The two-room efficiency was very cozy. The main room, which was used for eating, sleeping, and entertaining, was just big enough for two people to lie down.

In the apartment, all extraneous personal effects were stuffed in the closet and the natural focal point in the middle of the room was the *kotatsu* (table-heater). In ancient times, these were actually square firepits used to cook food and warm the dwelling. The modern equivalent is more like an upside-down space heater, covered by a comforter, which hangs beneath the table top. It was the middle of winter when I arrived, so the extra warmth was much appreciated.

DAILY LIFE

On the cold winter mornings, I set my alarm an hour early. Since the floor was literally made of straw, it was not safe to leave the heater on all night. I would stick my *do-gi* (uniform) under the comforter and catch another hour of sleep. The rest of the dawn ritual consisted of running outside (usually in my underwear) to turn on the gas, then returning to light the pilot and pump the water heater.

Taking a bath was another way to warm up. So, the next step was filling up the tub. As the level of the hot water slowly rose, it was customary to sit on a stool beside the tub to pre-wash. A small bucket was utilized to wash up, so one could be completely clean before entering the tub. Often, in each household the bath water would be left for the next person. Since I had different roommates each time I went to Japan, I made sure I was always first.

Back then, breakfast consisted of ramen noodles and eggs. Afterwards it was time to walk or ride bikes a little more than a mile to the *Dojo*. Tanemura Sensei's classes usually ran about two hours. But because the grandmaster never skimped on our training or instruction, class would sometimes continue beyond the scheduled ending point.

At that time of year, we could all see our breath when we entered the training hall. Those who had been warming up for a while had visible vapor rising from their bodies. Because of the cold, organized practice began with up to a thousand *daken kihon* (basic blocks and strikes). Each person would count out ten sets until we had exhausted the prescribed number.

Then we would proceed to do *ukemi gata* (breakfalls and rolls). Forward, backward, and sideways we tumbled and smashed ourselves to the mat. Right away, I noticed that Sensei's *tatami* were the hardest I had ever encountered. Later I found out that it had been packed down by over 30 years of continuous use. Suddenly, the senior student would shout a command and all action ceased. Grandmaster Tanemura had entered the *Dojo* and, as always, we bowed and took our places.

During the first month, I developed a partnership with a very talented martial artist from Israel. He'd been living in Japan for an extended period of time. Since we were preparing to test for the same level, Tanemura Sensei paired us up. He was especially helpful in two ways: first, his knowledge of the train system made it far easier for me to get around; and second, his time in the country and language skills made Tanemura Sensei's corrections and lectures far easier to understand.

A DIFFERENT DOJO

Back in those days, Tanemura Sensei taught in other Japanese towns too. So, I followed my teacher and attended classes in Urawa (city). After three trains and a long winter walk in the middle of a mostly concrete part of the city, I finally found the address. Winding through a dark alley, I ascended the five or six flights and came up to a dojo much different from the *Honbu Dojo* in Matsubushi Machi.

The communal *tatami* (mat) room was used by several different teachers. Black and white pictures of each historical founder hung from the wall on very long cords. Each portrait could be easily turned around so as not to offend the other traditions. After flipping over the iconic picture of Takamatsu Sensei holding a staff, Tanemura Sensei asked that someone fetch a box of matches.

As I came to find out, many Japanese structures are not centrally heated. This temporary training hall was no exception. The only source of warmth was a small Kerosene heater, which sat in a lonely corner of the room. After changing on the dojo floor into our *do-gi* and *hakama* (skirt-like pants), we warmed up with the usual series of rolls, break falls and daken kihon. – Many dojo in Japan do not have locker rooms, so men dress right on the tatami floor. The women usually change behind a screen, giving a semblance of privacy. –Afterwards, we lined up and recited the *Ninniku Seishin*.

Sensei, paired each of us according to level, and I again was partnered with my new friend from Israel. We were both working on *sandan* (third-degree black belt) but apparently I hadn't yet mastered the art of falling. Several times when I was thrown, I hit the ground with such force that the burning element inside the heater was extinguished. Tanemura Sensei, was not very happy with my performance but lightened the mood by asking, "Michael, are you getting fat?" I smiled politely and he explained that good falling is just as important as good throwing. After that I redoubled my efforts to try to fall as quietly as a cat.

A SUBWAY DRUNK

After the class, most of us went our separate ways. Tanemura Sensei had a large car, but I didn't yet have the seniority to ride in it. Therefore, I had to endure the cold walk back to the train station with a few of the other foreign students.

The subway was very crowded that night. It was after 9 p.m., but some "salary men" were just returning home from afterwork libations. I was carrying an unusually large backpack. The metro was so crowded, I must've disturbed several people every time I turned.

One particularly inebriated gentleman was more than slightly perturbed. Although he was only inches away from me, he chose to focus his aggression on a smaller Japanese man who was lucky enough to be sitting down and reading a newspaper. I couldn't pick up everything he said, but through his slurred and angry voice I could hear over and over his disgust with foreigners in his country.

As tensions grew, his movements became larger and more animated. The drunk was so frustrated that he actually slapped the newspaper out of the other man's hands. I immediately changed my grip on the handrail to a more defensive pose. At the same time, I shot a glance over to my fellow martial artists. They, also aware of the situation, silently asserted their willingness to give me assistance if necessary.

I'd never met this man before, but I was suddenly struck by some kind of recognition. When I saw his face, I could tell that this was not his normal way of acting. I believed that something was deeply troubling him, and that he over-indulged with alcohol to forget. Perhaps he really went too far, because at the time, it seemed that his normal spirit had left his body and another one had taken it over. But I couldn't tell for sure. I was only guessing. - In any case, the situation eventually calmed down.

A BOJUTSU TWO-PERSON DRILL

CODE OF CONDUCT

The code of conduct is *Banpen Fugyo*, the importance of self-composure. When any great incident occurs, from a massive typhoon to the longest of earthquakes, never be surprised or afraid. Control yourself and act according to your judgment. Following the code of conduct with "God's heart, God's eyes" leads naturally to the acquisition of self-composure.

In the past, Ninja were taught the way to avoid mental weakness. Self-composure is achieved by following three important principles (*Sanbyo no Imashime*).

1. Do not keep fear within one's heart. To overcome fear, develop an immovable heart.

2. Do not look at an adversary as an inferior. Be cautious with anyone who seems to be weak. Remember that there have been many cases where a weak man has suddenly become fierce. Use courage to do what is necessary.

3. Do not over think. When confronted by a situation, do not analyze it too much; by then it may be too late. The ideal is to do boldly what is necessary with the greatest possible care.

-Tanemura Shoto Sensei

TAKAMATSU SENSEI'S TRAINING

SHOTEN NO JUTSU

I started training in shoten no jutsu (running and climbing towards Heaven) when I was 13. At first, I used a plank 3 cm thick by two ken (an old Japanese unit of measurement two ken = about 4 meters) in length. I put it on a 45-degree angle and would run up it many times. Over time, this angle was gradually increased to 60 or 70 degrees. So in the end, I could run straight up at 90 degrees. Running up hills is also good training. In China, shoten no jutsu helped me escape from a gang of attackers. This ability and training saved my life more than once.

-Takamatsu Toshitsugu Sensei

KOPPO-JUTSU

Old style koppo-jutsu training was very difficult. These days, the following practices are not recommended but are presented for historical purposed. At first one would train the fingers and toes thrusting them repeatedly into sand. Next, small pebbles were used. Finally, the digits could stand to endure a bucket full of rocks. Of course, the nails and fingertips will flow with blood at first, and it would be extremely painful and difficult to persevere. But at last the joints become completely conditioned.

Takamatsu Sensei's succeeded in this type of severe training. His nails could not be cut by regular clippers; only by the pinchers used to trim Bonsai trees. His fingers were so strong that he could crack a table or a box just by extending his fingers straight out. In his later years, he admitted that this kind of hard practice can deform joints and is useless nowadays. I have the same opinion.

- Tanemura Shoto Sensei

GRANDMASTER TANEMURA'S QUEST FOR MEANING III

Many people are interested to know the future. They are excited about what's around the corner or how some plan is going to work out. From my experience I have learned that some important things seemed destined to be, and other predicted events can certainly be altered.

TANEMURA DIES AT EIGHTEEN

By my twelfth birthday, I was very good at fortune telling. I used various methods to tell friends, neighbors and family members exact details about their past, present and future. To my recollection, the facts I gave them never proved to be wrong. It was all very interesting and fun until I read my own fate. It seemed by all accounts that I was supposed to be dead by the age of eighteen! I checked and re-checked, but the signs all pointed to a very early funeral.

I knew that I was correct and that there was nothing that I could do to change it, so I decided to make the most of the few short years I had left. I started smoking and drinking heavily. I fought with street fighters. In short, I fully cultivated an "I don't give a damn" attitude and generally made a mess of my life. Luckily, I survived to see my eighteenth birthday, and shortly after those things came to a halt.

Some friends and I were in a car headed to Yokohama Bay. It was raining, but we didn't have a care in the world. From out of nowhere, a fire truck appeared and struck our vehicle broadside. The other passengers were thrown clear. I, on the other hand, was trapped in the backseat with the side door and window bashed in. The glass crushed against my face. The shock and loss of blood made me go unconscious. The lead officer mistakenly pronounced me "dead on the scene," and someone got in touch with my parents. An ambulance transported my body to the hospital.

In a white room, I woke up. I knew very well at that moment that I could have easily been looking at a white light instead. I was alive for a reason, and it wasn't just to have parties. I had already been studying martial arts for ten years, but for selfish reasons. I had been weak. Budo made me strong. But what good is strength if you can't use it to help others. I knew that I had to do more - I decided to become a policeman. I promised God that I would quit drinking and smoking and dedicate my life to fighting guilty guys.

Days later, I was released. My face bandaged and body bruised, I took a taxi home. I had forgotten my keys, so I knocked at the door. My mother answered, but she didn't recognize me.

"Who are you?"

"Your son, Tsunehisa."

"That's not funny young man! My son is dead. Can't you see that all of our relatives are gathered here for his funeral preparations?"

I looked past her incredulously, but soon my eyes confirmed that she was telling the truth. – "Mom!" I said with all seriousness and looked into her eyes. That was all it took. Painful weeping turned into tears of joy. My relations were both confused and relived.

- Tanemura Shoto Sensei

AMATSU TATARA SCROLLS

While the name Amatsu Tatara is not well-known even in Japan, the names of the secret scrolls and books based on the Amatsu Tatara tradition are recognizable to highly educated Japanese scholars, martial artists and spiritual experts. The existence of these *makimono* (scrolls) is well known to Ninpo martial artists of the Takamatsu lineage, but very little of this knowledge has been taught until now.

It is difficult to explain the Amatsu Tatara publicly because its knowledge has always been intended for only special grandmasters or priests, and thus it had been kept secret. I, Shoto Tanemura, am the 58th grandmaster of Amatsu Tatara *Bumon* (martial arts) and *Shumon* (spiritual arts). I feel that the time has come to show what the Amatsu Tatara truly is.

- Tanemura Shoto

AMATSU TATARA HIBUMI

Takamatsu Toshitsugu wrote about the Amatsu Tatara Hibumi (secret scrolls) in his Amatsu Tatara Budo Keizu Hikan scroll. The scrolls contain information about all martial arts, spiritualism and humanism.

KING MIMA

According to the tradition, the Amatsu Tatara Hibumi were written around 700 BC by the king of Mima as a record of the history of Japan. Empress Tatara Isuzu Hime no Mikoto was given these Scrolls as its ninth grandmaster. She then married the first emperor Jinmu and gave these scrolls to the Ohtomo, Nakatomi and Mononobe families who had close ties to the emperor.

At that time, these scrolls were made from the bark of the cedar tree. They were written in *Kamiyo Moji*, an ancient form of ideograms, which literally translates as "God's characters."

The story of king Mima was explained in the hand-written book Kuki Bunsho Kaisetsu in the chapter called Ama no Kami Matsuri and also in the Izumo Hisho secret scroll. Around 700 BC, King Mima drifted from an ancient Babylonian kingdom to Japan with three attendants and they came to live on Miwayama Mountain. King Mima was a prophet, philosopher, astronomer, and theologian. He formed a friendship with Amaterasu Ohmikami who was the chieftain of Japan and was making great efforts in controlling the country. This is why he was made a Kunitsu-Omi Muraji (minister).

King Mima brought with him a *Kubikazari* (special necklace) that was made of 72 *magatama* (jewels). The Kubikazari was not only for fashion, but also had a very important purpose as a tool for the prediction of future events. King Mima presented this Kubikazari to Amaterasu. All the Japanese "divine-kings" gathered at the center of Japan and chose Amaterasu as the emperor. From that moment on, the person who received the *Kubikazari* became the next emperor of Japan.

Around 500 BC, Several hundred Vedic Buddhists of the Malay decent sailed to Japan and attacked the emperor's army at Mount Miwayama. The Imperial army fought valiantly and defeated them. The invaders in turn apologized sincerely and asked for mercy. The emperor's heart was moved, so he actually permitted them stay in Japan and to live in the Shiki area. During this conflict, new weapons and techniques were designed and developed. They also developed military strategies.

ONE SCROLL BECOMES MANY

Around 10 AD a single scroll named Amatsu Tatara *Hibumi-no-Ikkan* (the single secret scroll of the Amatsu Tatara) was written. This scroll includes special techniques, philosophies, *tenmon* (astronomy and astrology studies), *chimon* (geological studies) and other strategies.

The Shinmei Shii no Hiden is a collection of four separate sets of scrolls that were based on the Amatsu Tatara *Hibumi-no-Ikkan*. The titles of these sets are explained in the Kumano Shugenja to Michishirube scroll as well as by Takamatsu Sensei's notes.

The main scroll was transmitted to the Nakatomi family as the Amatsu Tatara Nakatomi Hibumi (Kukami-Kuki Bunsho) and later this was passed on to the Kuki family. The Ohtomo family scrolls are known as the Amatsu Tatara Kishin no Hibumi (Ohtomo Bunsho); and the Abe family through Nagasunehiko as the Amatsu Tatara Rinpo Hiden (Oohikonaga-den, Abe Bunsho).

The 106 (or 127 by some counts) scrolls of these 4 families are collectively known as the Shinmei Shii-no-Hiden. In October of 1640, the third Shogun, Iemitsu Tokugawa, ordered a copy of these scrolls to be stored in the *Edo* (now Tokyo) castle treasury for safekeeping.

- Tanemura Shoto Sensei

MY APPROACH TO ANCIENT KNOWLEDGE

The current *Soke* is the only person to truly understand the full meaning of these historic documents. For me, it is enough to know that he is willing to share some of their secrets with those of us who are dedicated and work hard enough to deserve them. Most students can't even read basic Japanese, let alone the millennia old *Kamiyo Moji* (ancient script). What information Tanemura Sensei has transmitted so far, though, has been remarkably timeless and practical.

In ancient times (but also as recently as 150 years ago), most people had very few choices in life. Whatever station one was born into was where one stayed until death. Today, I believe that many of us have too many choices. Few commit themselves to anything, because it seems no longer necessary to stand up and be counted. Knowledge also has become cheap and easily accessible. Just mention any word and within seconds the internet can provide thousands of references.

Yet with all of the freedom and opportunities we enjoy, human beings have changed very little in 2,500 years. We still are born, grow up and die. We still want our bodies to be safe and our minds to be peaceful. I believe that the dedicated study of this art can accomplish both of these things. Today, because of ample leisure time and access to information, we have an even greater chance of success.

A BIKENJUTSU TECHNIQUE AGAINST A STAB (USING LIVE BLADES)

SANDAN TESTING

THE EXAM AND PUNISHMENT

At the Honbu Dojo in Japan, my Israeli training partner and I closed our eyes, mentally preparing for the test to come. The dojo had a chill, and the air was utterly silent. Eventually, we were standing face to face in front of the Grandmaster. Then, we bowed and began our arduous examinations for third degree black belt.

With determination and focus, we took turns throwing each other to the floor and slashing at each other with swords. Even though, we both performed exactly the same techniques, I received a lower score. Originally, Tanemura Sensei and his Shihan judged my performance at 97%, but because during one technique I threw my partner too close to the grandmaster, two points were deducted (95%).

Tanemura Sensei said, "If you're performing in front of the Emperor and your partner lands on him, no one will care how beautiful your technique looked." In any case, I had passed my *sandan* test.

The next day I entered the training hall elated and thought that I could do no wrong, at least in my own mind. I believe that Tanemura Sensei sensed this attitude, but began teaching me the new *yondan* (fourth degree) techniques anyway. It was February 1993, and up to this point everything had come fairly easily. The first two techniques passed without incident. My performance was decent, but my ego was swelling to dangerous proportions. Tanemura Sensei looked at me squarely and asked, "Do you think you know this technique?" Something about my attitude and eyes during my affirmative answer made the grandmaster very upset. I needed to be punished, so he explained that I no longer deserved to learn any new techniques. For 365 days, he kept his promise.

THE DEVELOPMENT OF THE FUTEN SHIBU
PART THREE

While Soke was teaching me some hard lessons, people from several foreign countries responded to my second article written about the Grandmaster published in an international martial arts magazine. Canada, Italy and Spain were only a few places that had interested potential students. More important to the Futen Dojo story are the nations in which I actually taught seminars.

Canada was the closest to my home. I didn't even have a passport the first time I went there. My birth certificate faxed to the airport got me over the border. The organizers asked me to bring several weapons with me. So, I ended up having to spend another two hours in Canadian Customs. Eventually, I did get there to teach. There were many questions and challenges to the effectiveness of our system. But, I was able to brave the cold and dispel the doubts with the help of Tanemura Sensei's teachings.

When I returned home from Canada, Tanemura Sensei temporarily named me the head of training in that country. These days, a different Genbukan instructor has that responsibility, although I do still have a few Canadian students.

After one student was allowed to fly over from Europe and train with me, I was invited to teach in Italy. With permission each time from Tanemura Sensei, this pattern was repeated several times. At one point back home, so many people were asking for extended stays, I rented a spare apartment to accommodate them. Over the years, many satellite schools have been set up in various countries.

Grandmaster Tanemura has students in over twenty countries. I feel honored to have practiced this martial art in places like Spain, Brazil, Chile, and Argentina among other nations. The message that he teaches truly speaks to people from many different cultures, languages and backgrounds.

YONDAN

"Those skilled in war bring the enemy to the field of battle. They are not brought there by him."
-Sun Tzu

CHAPTER IV

MEETING KIMURA SENSEI

In 1995, I was given the amazing opportunity to accompany Tanemura Sensei on a visit to see one of his teachers, Kimura Masaji Sensei. Kimura Sensei was an extraordinary martial artist. He happened to be one of Takamatsu Sensei's first and eldest students. There's no doubt that no other person had as much personal instruction from Takamatsu Sensei.

After being initiated into Takamatsu Sensei's dojo in 1917, Kimura Sensei continued to live very close to his Grandmaster until Takamatsu Sensei's death in 1972. After more than 55 years of almost continuous, daily training, Kimura Sensei was still able to execute techniques both unarmed and with weapons 28 years later. I personally experienced the master's almost magical techniques, when he was 95 years old!

DID I SEE A GHOST?

During the long train ride from *Tokyo* to the *Nara* area, I had time to wonder what Kimura Sensei would be like at such an old age...

Would he be physically able to talk with us? Would he be confined to a bed at a nursing home? Would his memory still be sharp enough to recount the secret details of his martial arts history?

After our arrival in southern Japan, Tanemura Sensei honored us with a solemn visit to the gravesite of Takamatsu Sensei. We paid our respects to the master in the traditional way.

I didn't know what to expect, so I watched quietly as Tanemura Sensei led me to this sacred site. The Grandmaster devoted much concentration to each and every action. First, Soke carefully washed the grave, something I had never seen done before. After the main area was finished, he removed and cleaned a teacup from a pedestal on the tombstone. Grandmaster Tanemura explained to me that it was actually Takamatsu Sensei's favorite drinking vessel. I was relieved to see that it had remained unbroken since his death in the early 1970's.

Next, I was allowed to light special incense and gently lay the smoldering sticks in a stone receptacle. As thin wisps of smoke rose skyward, we took a quiet moment to offer prayers and ask for guidance. When I opened my eyes, I was surprised to see a jovial Japanese gentleman walking towards me from the East. It was even more shocking because to my eyes, he looked exactly like Takamatsu Sensei!

While Tanemura Sensei offered his greetings to Kimura Sensei, I was temporarily dumbfounded. His resemblance to the late master and the location of the meeting added a surreal quality to the scene. To top it off, I was being introduced to the oldest living master of our Amatsu Tatara arts.

To illustrate his ever-present respect, Kimura Sensei removed his gray flannel hat, bowed and shook my hand. So, I in turn used my parasol to shade him from the sun as he walked over to Takamatsu Sensei's grave. The elder master then offered incense in the manner previously described. However, a very curious thing happened next.

Though Kimura Sensei offered even fewer sticks of scented embers than the rest of us, the effect seemed amplified. Remarkably, more copious amounts of smoke mysteriously started to billow forth from the small hearth. When Kimura Sensei bowed his head and joined his hands, it was as if the cinnamon-colored clouds were responding to his prayer.

THE MASTER WITH THE KINDEST HEART

Soon after leaving the cemetery, we were escorted to Kimura Sensei's family home to hear many of Takamatsu Sensei's *kuden* stories. As soon as we walked into his main parlor, Kimura Sensei proceeded to pick up and move furniture. We tried to stop him, but the elder master wouldn't hear of it. He was surprisingly strong and agile. All Tanemura Sensei and I could do was to follow his orders until Kimura Sensei finally came to rest in *seiza*.

For the next couple of hours, Kimura Sensei recounted dozens of training stories from his many decades with Takamatsu Sensei. All the while, the elder master remained unbelievably still. I tried to follow suit by suffering on my knees for what seemed like an eternity. But, of course I found that to be very difficult.

My legs fell asleep several times. The pins and needles sensation eventually forced me into a crossed-legged sitting position. On the other hand, Kimura Sensei never once appeared uncomfortable, like a rock formation. His stability seemed natural and relaxed. I doubt that very many people today could do as well.

Suddenly, my teacher's teacher became animated. He stood up quickly and showed Tanemura Sensei a new variation of a *Takagi Yoshin Ryu Jujutsu kata.* In the centuries-old technique called *Oikake Dori,* one usually approaches the opponent from behind. If all goes well, the *uke* (receiver) gets kicked in the calf muscle and pulled down to his back. Kimura Sensei showed what to do if your opponent strongly resists.

After trying unsuccessfully to pull Tanemura Sensei down, Kimura Sensei slipped his right arm under my teacher's left elbow and locked it; he continued with a reverse heel kick to Tanemura Sensei's shin; then he quickly swept his right leg back, which forced Sensei to flip forward (rather than suffer a broken leg); immediately, Kimura Sensei dropped down on one knee and executed a reverse *ura-ken* (back fist) to a special *kyusho* (pressure point) near Tanemura Sensei's sternum.

Needless to say, I was very impressed! Kimura Sensei continued to show techniques and counter strategies. Some throws were even performed on me. Gradually, I began to experience another level of martial arts. I believe that because Kimura Sensei understood the *kata* so well, his body automatically adjusted for the situation at hand. Even though this is not a new concept; it gains significance and importance being performed by someone with his age and experience.

"WHO'S THE BIGGEST GUY IN HERE?"

The most impressive demonstration, however, came at dinner that night. Tanemura Sensei had arranged a special meal for Kimura Sensei, some of my students and me in a private room at a traditional Japanese restaurant. We were all very excited and honored to be treated so warmly. As I introduced my students one by one, grandmaster Kimura remarked about how tall we all were compared to him.

The difference in our height reminded me of a technique Kimura Sensei performed earlier that day. The demonstration started with me attacking the older master in a common grappling position. Because I was comparatively large and difficult to throw using brute strength, Kimura Sensei did something utterly unexpected. In a flash, the master dropped across me at an odd-degree angle. This allowed him to unbalance and topple me immediately, using very little power. The technique really needs to be seen to be understood.

My thoughts were interrupted when Kimura Sensei called out, "Who's the biggest guy in here?"

One of my students (obviously over 200 pounds) stood up. Tanemura Sensei translated, telling my student that Kimura Sensei wanted him to participate in a test. For the sake of background, I would like to say that Kimura Sensei was 95 years old, not quite five feet tall and less than 100 pounds. My student was instructed to grab the grandmaster by the shoulders and try to force him back to the wall.

Up until that moment, I had the utmost confidence in Japanese *Ninpo* masters. However, in this case, I was a little concerned. Kimura Sensei had never met my student before. This particular opponent was not very experienced in the peaceful aspects of our martial arts. Also, he was known to have lost control on more than one occasion. But it was already too late for me to express any objections.

The oddly-matched pair stood poised in the middle of the room. We all backed away from our *miso* soup and gourmet sushi. Naturally, I positioned myself very close to the action.

Suddenly, my student's face turned serious. His muscles tightened as he hunched his back and pushed forward on the shoulders of the elder master with all of his might. Very soon, the attacker's facial expression changed to an interesting mixture of pain and delight.

Kimura Sensei had located a particular *kyusho* (pressure point) on my student's chest. He then used one carefully-placed finger to paralyze his aggressor, even forcing the larger opponent backwards.

The combatants hadn't moved more than a few inches, but the fight was already over. Afterwards, my student couldn't help but laugh at the fact that such an old man had bested him.

LESSONS FROM THE PAST

The rest of the night was less physical, but still educational. The master told us about Takamatsu Sensei's younger days and the serious training he had undergone. Kimura Sensei said that when he first started to study, he was only interested in learning techniques that worked in real situations. Many times, he would spar with Takamatsu Sensei, only to be quickly beaten.

With every class and each loss, Kimura Sensei gained new insight into himself as a person as well as a martial artist. He explained that Takamatsu Sensei taught in a very traditional manner. But in addition, Takamatsu Sensei emphasized that the kata by themselves were not enough. One had to be able to utilize them in terms of *jissen-jutsu* (real life fighting). To both masters, this was the realization of true *Budo*.

Kimura Sensei was the first student to receive a *menkyo kaiden* from Takamatsu Sensei, and this was in *Tenshin Hyoho Kukishin ryu*.

While this art is connected to the *Kukishin ryu* Tanemura Sensei learned from Sato Kimbei Sensei, it was also unique in many ways. Kimura Sensei showed *kamae* (stances), techniques, and *kuden* for the *bojutsu*, *hanbojutsu* and *bikenjutsu* never before seen. My teacher, Tanemura Sensei, later remarked that the *Tenshin Hyoho kata* are rare patterns from the Japanese Edo period and that they taught many secrets. For example, how to defeat an aggressive swordsman.

However, the most important thing to understand is that the real purpose of the Amatsu Tatara arts is for us to find true peace and happiness. From my observations, Kimura Sensei appeared to be one of the happiest people I've ever met. Perhaps some of us will be fortunate enough to experience joy and fulfillment as long.

PRESERVATION OF SPIRITUAL HEALTH

There are two main creeds to preserve spiritual health: Yojo Shiketsu and Hasshodo. The four main points that they teach to preserve health are:

Avoid anger to preserve a steadfast heart. Being patient requires more effort than becoming angry. With humility, develop your personality.

Avoid excessive worrying to preserve the nerves. Don't spend too much time thinking

about trivial matters, otherwise you will become irresolute. Worry less and develop strong nerves.

Avoid excessive speaking to preserve the spirit. Refrain from jabbering too much so as to store up the power of your spirit.

Avoid desire to preserve the heart. The problems of the mind are usually expressed as desire: "I want this... I want that... or I want to be rich and belong to the upper class, etc." Try hard to avoid such desires and, instead, cultivate a good mind and heart.

-Takamatsu Toshitsugu Sensei

THE AUTHOR TEACHING IN ITALY

LEARNING THE RESPONSIBILTY OF BEING A TEACHER

The 1995 trip to Japan was the first time I brought students along with me to the Land of the Rising Sun. The 95°F/35°C temperatures and stifling humidity were in stark contrast to my winter training at the *Honbu Dojo* the first time I came. Even though everyone in the group was an adult, as *dojo-cho* it still proved to be my responsibility to look after and even rescue my students.

The night before we were all to board the train to Kyoto, one of my students lost his travel wallet! His passport and all of his money were inside. Of course, Tanemura Sensei refused to leave without locating it. The Grandmaster has shown me many times through his compassionate and careful actions that being a Sensei is akin to being a father. We take care of our children even when they, themselves are careless.

It was already dark before I was aware of the situation. And, to complicate matters, it started to rain. I was only dressed in my pajamas when I got the call to search the road in the darkness. With an umbrella in one hand and a flashlight in the other, I searched the weeds, rice fields and ditches alongside the road.

Earlier that evening, the town had hosted a small festival and the left-over paper lanterns provided a bit more illumination. After about an hour, Tanemura Sensei surprised me. As I walked with my head down, the Grandmaster pulled up from behind in his wife's car. With a comforting smile, he explained that someone had found the travel wallet and taken it to the police station. I immediately joined Tanemura Sensei and my student and headed to the law enforcement office. Tanemura Sensei felt that it would be a worthwhile experience for me to learn first-hand how to fill out a Japanese police report.

The next day we got up bright and early and reached Ueno Train Station without incident. After transferring to the *Shinkansen* (bullet train), we had only a few minutes to find our seats and get settled. Another one of my students decided that he was thirsty and went back to the platform to locate a vending machine. I'll never forget the look on his face as the train pulled away. Out of desperation, he actually ran beside the train for a few yards. I didn't know what to do.

For a moment I considered pulling the emergency stop chord. Later Sensei explained that every minute the train is delayed carries a fine of over $10,000. I looked to my teacher for guidance, but he simply referred to my student as, "Unbelievable!" and seemed uninterested.

I glanced over at Soke a few times. I was flabbergasted, but he still remained silent and seemed to be focused on the book he had brought along. Eventually, Tanemura Sensei rose from his seat and left the cabin car. Soke returned with a bottle of his favorite tea. It turns out the train had a dining car, which made my student's action seem even more unnecessary.

We arrived in Kyoto, and I still had no idea where my student was. Tanemura Sensei ordered us to stay at the platform and didn't return for almost thirty minutes. Presently, another train from Tokyo arrived. To our great surprise, a female train attendant came walking off escorting my student. She delivered him with a bow, then re-boarded the train.

Finally, I realized that without my knowledge, Tanemura Sensei had contacted Ueno station and arranged for my student to be escorted onto the next train. I realized that my anxiety was counterproductive and that within the first few minutes my teacher had calmly handled the situation. Not all lessons are learned in the dojo.

GRANDMASTER TANEMURA'S QUEST FOR MEANING IV

A VERY BAD FEELING ABOUT TOMORROW

"Captain, Sir?"

"Yes, Tanemura-san."

"I had a terrible dream last night that involved you and our entire police squad."

The Captain was very familiar with my *Ninpo* background. Though he didn't believe absolutely everything I said, he knew that I had been right about many things in the past.

"Tell me all the details of what you think is going to happen, and I will speak to some of my colleagues," he said with honest concern.

My commanding officer was sympathetic, but not all of the law enforcement personnel at the Tokyo Metropolitan Police Department treated me nicely. Ever since the academy, my skills and patience were constantly tested.

CHALLENGERS COME BECAUSE OF HIS REPUTAION

As beginning police cadets (and throughout the length of our public service) we were required to study, among other things, *judo*, *kendo* and *taiho-jutsu* (full-contact police self-defense). My prior *ninpo*, *jujutsu* and *bikenjutsu* training made it difficult for my classmates to beat me even in a sports competition fight. So gradually, as rumors of my "ninja" abilities spread, challengers started to attack without warning.

One of the most memorable instances happened while I was walking alone through the academy courtyard. A future police officer jumped out from behind the bushes and attacked me with a sword. I escaped his initial attack and rolled to my feet, but immediately he was poised to strike again.

"If you come at me a second time, I will have to kill you!" I said with all seriousness. For a moment, we were both motionless as he searched my eyes. Finally, the cadet thought better of it and yielded without further delay.

AN UNLIKELY STUDENT

Closer to and after graduation, I had many more encounters with other law enforcement personnel who wanted to test me in various ways. One even ended up becoming a good friend and *deshi* (student disciple).

"Hajime!" the *Kendo* judge yelled as a signal to start the match.

My opponent out-ranked me by several degrees of black belt in modern fencing but had never beaten me in a sparring bout. Using traditional sword techniques, I scored points very quickly. My adversary and fellow cadet was extremely upset and confused.

"Kochira kachi desu!" the official said loudly as he motioned towards me. After only a couple of minutes, I had been announced the winner.

We bowed ceremoniously to each other, then the referee, and I turned to walk away. Without warning, my classmate attacked me from behind with his sword. The next thing I knew, my shinai was at his throat. Even though this was not the first time that he had tried something unexpected, I could see the surprise in his eyes all the way through the metal grill of his *men* (facemask).

Like something out of a movie, he immediately genuflected and asked me to accept him as a student.

Of course, my initial response was no. Not just because of his aggressive actions, I could also see clearly that his heart had a dark color around it. At that time, I couldn't imagine how I could do anything to change him. But he was persistent.

For six months, he brought me towels and water after practice. He called me Sensei and showed me the respect usually given to a master. For my part, I tried not to pay him much attention; rather I looked inwardly at his heart. I wanted to see his real intentions and if his spirit had changed.

To my surprise, in half a year, he had truly grown up. I decided to start a Ninpo club at the police station, and he was one of the first members. Also, I was glad not to have to worry anymore about him trying to attack me from behind while we walked the neighborhoods in our police uniforms

SERIOUS TROUBLE AT THE AIRPORT

"Tanemura-san."

"Yes Sir, Capitan!"

"I've spoken to some of the other commanders. – I am the only one who completely believes you. Therefore, I will re-position the police squad as you suggested, but I can't say what they will do."

"Thank you for your trust, Sir."

"I do hope that you are wrong about this one."

"So do I, Sir."

Our assignment was to guard the construction of the Narita Airport, near Tokyo. Violent threats had been issued by militant groups, so at that time the site looked more like a military exercise field than an international hub of transit. Over the weeks and months several police officers had been injured.

The aggressors used everything from simple hand-held projectiles (like Molotov cocktails) to full-fledged grenade launchers. When we got to the area, we took up positions in our new strategic location. Then we went about our business as usual.

There was a lot of hustle and bustle. The bulldozers and trucks were working nonstop, and anti-riot squads were constantly patrolling. Suddenly, everything seemed eerily familiar. The background noise grew quieter and many things happened exactly the way I saw them in my dream. The only thing that had changed was that my group was in a different spot.

Then a burning and hissing sound erupted from one side. We all ducked automatically as a missile flew high above our heads. I couldn't believe it myself, even though I was watching it all happen. For a moment, all we could do was stand motionless and follow its movement with our eyes. "Boom!" The bomb exploded and we all snapped back to reality. The missile struck exactly where our squad would have previously been stationed. My commander and I said nothing more about it, because the implications were clearly understood. We had a job to do and thank Heaven we were all alive to do it.

A NEW MISSION

After fourteen years on the force and achieving the rank of Lieutenant, I had to retire from law enforcement. I learned many things on the job and really put all of my physical and mental skills to the test. I used *ninpo taijutsu* countless times to defend myself as well as others against drunks and drug addicts, and I explored the depths of the human psyche working in various ways against the *Yakuza* (Japanese Mafia). But I felt strongly that by the age of 37, my luck would have run out if I had stayed. I found a new mission: to teach this martial art and spiritual philosophy to the world.

- Tanemura Shoto Sensei

GRANDMASTER TANEMURA PERFORMING TANDOKU-
GATA (SOLO PRACTICE) WITH A SWORD

YONDAN TESTING

Fourth degree was in many ways a turning point in my understanding of Japanese martial arts. Because of the certifications necessary to qualify as a master of these arts, I was tested no fewer than five different ways at this level. Also, I came to see *ninpo* and *jujutsu* in a different light. Genbukan Ninpo Bugei and Kokusai Jujutsu Renmei, though headed by the same person, developed clear lines of demarcation.

Before 1991, the black belt levels included techniques from many different family traditions, and to me, it was not clear where the influence of one began and ended. As I entered the higher levels (starting with the Yagyu Shingan *Ryu*) I learned, for example, that some schools start their bowing on the left knee quietly and others salute with the right first accompanied by a loud slap on the ground. These differences were neither right nor wrong, but if one was to claim true mastery in a particular school they needed to be understood.

Tanemura Sensei had a rather daunting task: the Grandmaster wanted to make sure that thousands of people in countries all over the world learn the practical nature of these arts without losing the *Yamato no Kokoro* (the true spirit of ancient Japan).

I PASS IN JAPAN

A year earlier, I received my first *yondan* (forth degree black belt) license from Tanemura Sensei. This level was based upon my prior experience in the combined Genbukan School. Sensei had taught me certain complete patterns, but it wasn't until this trip to Matsubushi *Machi* (town) that I was tested on the official Kokusai Jujutsu Renmei material. The first test consisted of *waza* from three separate *jujutsu* schools; the second test was for Asayama Ichiden *Ryu*.

I was first exposed to the Asayama Ichiden *Ryu* techniques in 1988. They are direct and very practical. In one defensive example, the practitioner immediately disables whatever the opponent uses to attack. Fingers, wrists and elbows are but a few of the joints that are locked and controlled. The same could be said of many traditions, but what sets this school apart are the unique angles and innovative use of leverage.

In the Asayama Ichiden *Ryu*, surprise and body dynamics make the techniques extremely difficult to counter. As a police officer, Tanemura Sensei utilized these concepts hundreds of times in actual fighting situations, and I've seen the Grandmaster teach Western law enforcement personnel with great success. I passed both examinations and received certification and a special *densho* (secret book) from the Asayama Ichiden *Ryu* lineage.

I FAIL IN AMERICA

Because of my childish egoism and naïve lack of good judgment, my third test at *yondan* level ended in failure. It was during a Tai Kai in America and the organizer graciously agreed to schedule a private hour for me. Unless Tanemura Sensei comes specifically to my dojo, these one-on-one sessions with the Grandmaster come at a premium.

Some of the techniques that I was to perform involved multiple attackers. So, more than one of my students accompanied me. I was very aware of the minutes ticking by. So, I thought, to save time I asked one of them to help me take notes… As Tanemura Sensei evaluated my performance, he mentioned several points of correction. My student faithfully recorded his words. The Grandmaster suddenly realized my grave error and exclaimed, "Do you think you are a king? Your students are not servants or secretaries. – If you want to learn you must take your own notes!" With that Tanemura Sensei slammed his book closed, and it would be some time before I would get another opportunity.

TANEMURA SENSEI DEMONSTRATING A
KORYU KARATE KATA (FORM)

I GET A SECOND CHANCE

A year later, with some trepidation, I bowed to the Grandmaster. Several masters from Japan flanked him including Okayasu Shihan and Nagamoto Shihan (now deceased). These were Tanemura Sensei's best students.

Virtually every other instructor in the United States was also present, and the situation was very different than the time before. After the last technique - which involved throwing blinding powder in the faces of two sword-wielding attackers and disappearing - I sat by myself in the middle of the mat. After Soke passed his judgment, each of the Shihan were given the opportunity to critique my performance. Afterward, Tanemura Sensei read my score aloud. It was 98%, and this time I was sure to prepare and edit my own notes.

RENSHI TEST

The fifth and final test I took at my *yondan* level is described by Tanemura Sensei in the introductory manual this way:

Renshi : *"Line-up Master" or "Journeyman Master"*

Pre-qualifications : *Yondan Ninpo, Yondan Jujutsu,* and *Shoden Menkyo* in Asayama Ichiden R*yu.*

Test : The student sits in *seiza* (traditional kneeling posture) facing Soke with eyes open, calmly awaiting Soke's cut. Soke assumes *Daijodan no kamae* (over-head posture) with a *shinai* (bamboo sword) and when he feels the student is ready, he executes his choice of cuts. Soke selects which strike he will perform during the test to ensure authenticity. The student must completely escape without being hit.

My personal experience with this examination in Japan began with a simple question.

"Tanemura Sensei, could you please watch me perform this technique?"

"Please continue training Michael," he said without looking at me.

Then something changed. It felt like the whole room had moved up to a different altitude. The Grandmaster turned slowly, leveled his glance directly at me and studied my posture with his 'severe' eyes.

"I have been watching you all of the time, as I have been perceiving everyone in this room," he started with an almost too calm voice. "Right now, you are working as a partner with my son, Kotaro. If either of you does anything that might severely injure the other, I will certainly stop you. However, to assume that I am not paying attention is a great insult."

"Sensei, gomen nasai (I'm very sorry)."

I certainly was sorry, but I didn't quite understand his mood. As the class went on for another hour, the bar seemed to have been raised for all of us. Apparently, this kind of thing had happened before, because each member of the Honbu Dojo seemed to naturally become more focused and serious.

SWORD TEST

"Take your positions for the *Renshi* test!" Tanemura Sensei announced loudly at the end of class. The Shihan took their places at the east end of the room, and the other students crowded together on the west wall. The Grandmaster selected a bamboo sword, while I was directed to wait in meditation in the middle of the dojo.

When I opened my eyes, I was face-to-face with Soke. I had never seen this test before, so I was flying blind. – His sword was already raised, and I had no conscious way of knowing which cut the Grandmaster would choose. – My mind was clear, and I stared into his eyes unblinkingly. – Time disappeared; so did fear and anticipation.

The next thing I remember, it was over. I was sitting calmly in *seiza* about eight feet west of my former position. Tanemura Sensei had attacked me, my body had escaped, and I was waiting patiently for whatever happened next.

"Yoshi!" Sensei said with a confident grin.

Soke looked over toward his master-level students. Almost imperceptibly, they all quietly nodded their approval and confirmation. The training that preceded made it seem effortless. This is much more than I can say for the spiritual tests that followed. In any case, I had experienced the calm before the storm.

THE DEVELOPMENT OF THE FUTEN SHIBU PART FOUR

Sometimes as a volunteer and other times to supplement my income, I taught classes outside of my dojo. Schools and hospitals were where I had the most success, but I also did charity work for whoever really needed me. For five years I taught self-defense for free at a high school. Women's rape prevention was next, and a recommendation from the local Chief of Police got me a job instructing at one of the most sought-after prep schools in the state.

THE HAVES

The children of the richest parents in my city frequently attend this prestigious school. They seemed to have every advantage in addition to being well-connected. To their credit, most of my students there were sincerely smart and respectful. In any case, it's helpful and important for any child to take make use of these opportunities to learn what's not always taught in school. – It was a wonderful environment for education, and I was forced to articulate many aspects of the art in a more concise and cerebral way. – I was challenged intellectually.

THE HAVE NOTS

The inner city of Milwaukee is a very different side of town. The population I worked with there was 100% African American. They were classified as "at risk youth" because of, among other things, their high drop-out rate, instances of violence and startling numbers of teenage pregnancies. Kids, who don't feel like they have much of a future, usually fail to plan for one.

There were no multi-million-dollar ice-hockey rinks or Porches in the circular drive. But some things struck me as being the same. Both groups of children laughed at the same points in the demonstrations. The wrist escapes still worked as smoothly, and the questions about how I got started training with the Grandmaster were very similar. Nonetheless, as anyone would expect, their life experiences differed greatly.

Generally, I was challenged more physically in the inner-city environment. Even so, the "haves" and the "have nots" of the world both have a wonderful potential for growth and development in this martial art. As evidence, I have personally witnessed that children who've grown up in either environment have still gone on to become wonderful Genbukan teachers.

HELPING AT A PSYCHIATRIC HOSPITAL

"As that mental patient sat in the movie theater, I didn't know what was going through his mind!" began one of the Resident Care Technicians (RCT) at a state-run psychiatric facility where I was about to work.

"It wasn't even a violent film… more like something Disney would make… But anyway, he must've been really bothered by something that he saw. It took more than one of us to control him, when he suddenly became violent!"

That was the first story I was told about the man I'll call "Charles" (it's against the law for me to reveal his real name). Many more incidents followed, like the time he used his fingernails to injure a nurse during a sponge bath, or how he hurt several others with his bare hands. This man had been institutionalized in excess of 20 years and had harmed over 40 staff members. – They needed help to control him!

HE LOOKED LIKE A VAMPIRE

I was wearing a business suit when I arrived at the treatment center. I was looking for the Intensive Treatment Program (ITP) in an electronically locked area of the multi-structure complex. I was hired to teach non-violent defense and control techniques to a group of ten hospital personnel. They all volunteered to work with difficult cases such as Charles'.

Many types of disabilities were treated there, so some of the residents were less dangerous than others. On one occasion, I shared the hall with over fifteen little people. Their energy and walking pattern was so foreign to me, that I found myself getting caught up in it. I felt so off-balance that I had to grab the handrail that lined the walls in order to keep from stumbling.

When I finally found the proper building, I met my guide and was buzzed through security. I felt slightly claustrophobic when the doors locked behind me. The common area was cheery enough, complete with a card table. But nothing I had seen could really prepare me for my first visit with Charles.

His room was almost bare, with just a bed, a chair and a desk. If there was more, I couldn't make it out, because the room was very dark. Only small points of sunlight penetrated the room from behind the closed window shades. Charles' skin was sickly and pale from lack of exposure to the sun. Also, his overgrown nails were turning yellow. To me he looked like a vampire.

More than six feet-four and 250 pounds, he was big and very strong. From reading his report, I learned that he was 33 years old and had been institutionalized for at least 20 years. He was securely bound to the bed (hands close to his waist) with padded leather restraints that held him upright. In the beginning, I didn't understand why all the precautions were necessary, but later I was glad that they were firmly in place.

"Are you a new doctor?" he asked rather innocently, no doubt because of how I was dressed. I told him the truth and that I was there to help some of the staff members.

Luckily, the program I created for them worked very well. It utilized *ma-ai* (distance awareness), *taisabaki* (body movement and evasion) and *goshinjutsu* (practical self-defense) I learned from Tanemura Sensei to predict and control his attacks. The first program was so successful; they invited me back to teach more of their staff members.

Eventually, with the help of some very experienced co-workers, I literally re-wrote the book on their procedures and tactics. Many of their protocols were dangerous and ineffective. My Ninpo training helped me to quickly figure out why a particular strategy wasn't working and explain how to fix it.

OTHER PROGRAMS

I was also able to apply ancient teachings to help hospitalized children. I taught breathing exercises and therapeutic movement to anorexic teenagers, who the psychologists told me, in ten minutes of doing martial arts "opened up more than in three months of psychotherapy." I am constantly amazed at how many positive applications these Genbukan arts have.

GODAN

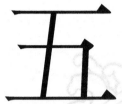

"When the thunderclap comes, there
is no time to cover the ears."
- Sun Tzu

CHAPTER V

NEVER TRY TO GO AROUND YOUR TEACHER

When I was 23 years old, by the grace of my teacher, I met one of Tanemura Sensei's teachers, Sato Kimbei Sensei. Of course, I was very honored and happy. I had the chance to train with one of my master's teachers once before, but Sato Sensei was even more intriguing than the first.

During the instructor's class, Sato Sensei was very open and extremely precise. Among many other things, Dr. Sato was a physician and expert in *kappo* (the art of resuscitation). More than just CPR, this art is an exhaustive study of the border between life and death. Safety precautions were given for both the would-be paramedic as well as the patient/opponent. Because of one simple fact: it is supremely difficult to save someone's life that is at the same time trying to cause you great harm.

The older Grandmaster, through my Sensei, spoke to me many times that week. He encouraged me to be a good student of Tanemura Sensei and to continue my studies, especially in Chinese martial arts. In addition, Sato Sensei even used me to demonstrate some basic postures, striking my body and kicking my legs to test the strength of my stances.

After returning to Japan, Sato Sensei's student set up a line of communication with me that didn't involve my direct teacher. That was a very bad idea. At first, I thought that it was an innocent thing. But later, Tanemura Sensei explained to me that it was not the proper protocol to "go behind him" to contact Sato Sensei. After he explained the bad manners and distrust it represented, I understood clearly why it was wrong. I should never have contacted this person directly.

I was very ashamed and embarrassed at my error. However, I was very lucky to have such an understanding teacher. Tanemura Sensei accepted my heart-felt apology. Later I found out that I would have been immediately expelled from the Genbukan had I continued.

INTRODUCTION

The most important thing when training in *Ninpo* is *Seishinteki Kyoyo* (spiritual refinement). Every martial art has its own form of spiritual guidance but in *ninpo*, if the spirit is not correctly developed with utmost care, a practitioner might accidentally kill someone or use the techniques of self-defense for a crime. Compared to other martial arts, the practitioner of *ninpo* needs a more refined sprit, a purer heart and harder physical training.

Within the Genbukan Dojo, there are various tests to analyze a student's character, wisdom, and above all mind control. The tests are not merely focused on the student's mastery of techniques. For instance, in the test for *Kyoshi* (master teacher) given only to above *godan* students, the student sits in the center of the *dojo* in front of the other pupils, and I as *Soshi* (Grandmaster) stand behind the student with a *shinai* (bamboo sword) above my head. Striking down towards the student's head with all my power but as silently as possible, I emit my *sakki* (killing intent). If my student is able to perceive this intent and consequently evades the *shinai*, he has passed the test and awarded the title *Kyoshi*. Only then can he be considered a true martial artist.

-Tanemura Shoto

TAKAMATSU SENSEI, REST IS IMPORTANT TOO

"Every day I am punctually in bed at nine o'clock with my pet cat to whom I have appointed the name of Jiro. I awake at half past six in the morning and take an ice water massage. Something that I haven't missed doing once in the past forty years and is why I have never been sick in bed. I enjoy painting very much and even now I continue painting as a form of play. I am not skillful, but still, I enjoy it. It's a pleasure for me."

- Takamatsu Toshitsugu, 1966

TANEMURA SENSEI MEETS FUKUMOTO YOSHIO SENSEI

Born in the winter of 1921, Fukumoto Yoshio Sensei was a friend of my father and had deep ties to me for generations. He lived very close in Noda City, and was a doctor specializing in bone disorders. He was originally from Shiga Prefecture and was the oldest son of a Wakamiya Shrine Shinto Priest.

Under the direction of Ueno Takashi Sensei, Master Fukumoto entered our *Bumon* and *Shumon* gate. By 1960, his sincere heart and strong techniques had grown, so his teacher allowed him to join training with Takamatsu Sensei's dojo in Nara. He eventually received *menkyo* and *kuden* in several traditional schools including: Amatsu Tatara Hiden, Tenshin Ryu *Kenpo*, Asayama Ichiden Ryu, Shinden Fudo *Ryu daken- taijutsu*, Togakure *Ryu ninpo*, Koto *Ryu koppo-jutsu* and Gyokko *Ryu kosshi-jutsu.*

By his own will, Fukumoto Sensei decided to keep his training a well-guarded secret. Even I didn't know everything until one day when I went to visit him. That morning, it felt to me as is if he were welcoming home his own child. He was so kind.

After we sat down, he took a long look at my face. Then he closed his eyes and went into a meditative state. I was quiet the whole time. A while later he opened his eyes again and began saying these words: "I started to study under Takamatsu Sensei in Showa 35 (1960). From him, I received *densho* (secret books), legends, and ancient scrolls. To this day, I have never allowed anyone see them or know of their existence. For you, I will show and give all of this, for I received a spiritual communication. This is the same kind of experience that occurred with Ueno Sensei."

Again, I was struck by the power of martial art destiny. Again, I felt the freshness of this truth and a renewed sense of purpose. He shared many kuden and hiden from Takamatsu Sensei. - Everything that Fukumoto Sensei did was done with sincerity. I believe that if one humbly strives and travels on this path with honesty, the light of *Shikin Haramitsu Daikomyo* naturally comes.

TAKAMATSU SENSEI IS TESTED

"Fukumoto-san pick up that metal sword!" Takamatsu Sensei ordered. Fukumoto Sensei began to become nervous with anticipation, but he did as he was told. It was a *shinken* (sharp sword) and he didn't want to kill his teacher. "When I turn my back and sit down, cut me at anytime."

Fukumoto Sensei raised the blade above his head, but he was so scared that his hands started shaking. Takamatsu Sensei sensed his hesitation and understood the doubt in his student's mind, even so, he told Fukumoto Sensei to redouble his efforts.

Finally, the *deshi* (disciple) worked up the enormous courage and stuck down silently with all his might. – But Takamatsu Sensei had already disappeared. The next thing Fukumoto Sensei knew, he was sent flying and had been simultaneously disarmed. He had no idea how his master had escaped.

Let me tell this to my students: the way of Amatsu Tatara equals the way of naturalness. A sincere heart will support and carry you as you walk this difficult road. If you keep the correct way, you too can truly know and get this experience.

-Tanemura Shoto Sensei

Before he died in 1995, Fukumoto Sensei passed all kuden and densho he earned from Grandmaster Takamatsu Toshitsugu and Grandmaster Ueno Takashi (including the final kuden of Togakure Ry*u*) to Tanemura Shoto Sensei.

GRANDMASTER TANEMURA'S QUEST FOR MEANING PART V

Finally, it happened! In the late 1960's, Tanemura Sensei was given a chance to meet Takamatsu Sensei. The journey from his home in Saitama Prefecture, in the days before high-speed "bullet" trains, took over twenty hours. But more than just distance kept them from meeting earlier. Grandmaster Tanemura has always believed in maintaining the proper student-teacher relationship. He knew about and had heard amazing stories concerning Takamatsu Sensei, but he would never dream of seeking him out without the consent and accompaniment of his Sensei at that time. Just because one can do something, doesn't mean that one should.

In the ancient traditions, if a student tried to go around his current master in favor of that person's teacher, he would receive "*hamon*." Similar to the concept of excommunication, the student would be expelled from the *dojo*, his name would be erased from the register and all rank taken away. Usually, no legitimate master would accept the student, once he had been blacklisted in this way. I didn't know about or understand this rule, until I almost found out the hard way.

TANEMURA SENSEI IS TAUGHT DIRECTLY

It is one thing to hear stories of warrior prowess, quite another to see it for oneself.

"... I'm getting on in age now and I don't remember all of the details." Takamatsu Sensei started after being asked a question about the old days. "I do recall, however, decapitating someone in Mongolia. He was one of a group a bandits on horseback. From my experience, I've learned that even if a large group of thugs attack, one only has to kill a few of them for the rest to turn tale and run."

Takamatsu Sensei had a great love for peace. Perhaps this devotion to non-violence had its roots in overcoming countless, life-threatening situations in his past.

"Our *Ninpo* is *Jissen-jutsu* (real life-protection) for the body and spirit!" said the Master emphatically. "Tanemura-san come here."

"Hai, Sensei!" the young Tanemura said without hesitation.

Like a dream come true, he faced the legendary *Budoka* (martial artist). Tanemura Sensei never explained to me exactly what happened next, but there is a picture of the outcome. In the photograph, the old master is mounted on top of his helpless student, choking him. Later, my teacher did eventually describe what he felt at that moment. "It was like he was holding me down by more than just his body weight. His *Ki* was in control in a way that I had never experienced before." His spirit bound along with his collar, and Takamatsu Sensei literally had Tanemura Sensei's life in the balance. Even after he was released, the junior *budoka* sensed the master in touch with him.

"YOU WILL BE A GREAT MASTER"

Some time later, Tanemura Sensei received a post from someone that had never written to him before. Grandmaster Takamatsu had some things to say that would change the young police officer's life forever. - *"You will be a great master."* Those six words written by Takamatsu Toshitsugu Sensei in his letter were enough to see my master through some very dark and confused times in his life.

By 1972, a great light had rejoined the heavens as Takamatsu Sensei passed away, and Tanemura Sensei naturally followed his distant cousin, the 34th grandmaster of *Togakure Ryu Ninpo*. For a while, things seemed hopeful. The training and teaching started to progress just as Takamatsu Sensei intended. But after several years, things began to change.

By 1984, Tanemura Sensei had received full mastership in everything that his teacher could give him. Having those *menkyo kaiden* licenses and his experience gave him the knowledge and authority to start his own organization. The Genbukan World Ninpo Bugei Federation was founded in 1984.

Soke Tanemura rededicated his life to teaching these arts the traditional way. Though he was a true grandmaster already, his days as a student were definitely not over. He had not yet realized Takamatsu Soke's full vision.

THE TRUE NINJA REVEAL THEMSELVES

The Iga and Koga mountains were the historical birthplace of some of our martial arts in Japan. I was fortunate enough to accompany Tanemura Sensei to this area one summer. Interested in capitalizing on the fame of the ninja, the town is now a major tourist attraction. From the moment we arrived at the train station, everything was *"shinobi no mono"*. The first thing I saw was some kids laughing and snapping photographs. They were taking turns sticking their heads through a hole. A black clad ninja was painted on the other side of the wood screen.

More important historical landmarks included a castle marking the spot where the infamous and unbelievably ruthless Oda Nobunaga planted his flag when he conquered the region. And, we also explored one of the most popular attractions, the Ninja House. This residence was moved intact from another part of Japan. Like its name suggests, the architecture included many trap doors and secret passageways. Today it sits atop a museum dedicated to the art of stealth, complete with scrolls, weapons and all manner of ninja gadgets. One of the main points that Tanemura Sensei emphasized was, "the moment one can say that it is a Ninja house, its ceases to be one."

In keeping with this concept, most of Takamatsu Sensei's grandmaster-level students chose to remain silent about their special training. Sato Sensei, Kimura Sensei, Fukumoto Sensei, and Kobyashi Sensei all continued practicing martial arts, but even Tanemura Sensei was ignorant of their connection to master Takamatsu until he was ready. Dr. Kimbei Sato taught at the Tokyo Metropolitan Police Academy while my teacher was a student there. They met at that time, but only after twenty years more did Sato Sensei reveal the depth of his knowledge.

In Takamatsu Sensei's hometown, things happened a little differently. Sometime after grandmaster Tanemura met with the Takamatsu Sensei's widow, Kimura Sensei miraculously revealed himself. My teacher had paid his respects at the Takamatsu family gravesite many times. It is only a stone's throw away from Kimura Sensei's house. But in all the years and visits before, the man who began his ninpo training in 1917 remained invisible. However, there is a famous saying, "When the student is ready, the teacher will appear." So, after my teacher had learned all he could from his relation, the old master made his presence known.

Fukumoto Sensei (as discussed earlier in this chapter) knew Tanemura Sensei's father for many years and lived within a few miles of Matsubushi Machi. Even so, Grandmaster Tanemura again had to be patient.

THE GRANDMASTER IS TESTED

Personally, of all the students of Takamatsu Sensei that I had the pleasure of meeting or of which I have heard stories, Kobayashi Masao Sensei sounded the most frightening. As is the custom,

Tanemura Sensei was invited to the master's study for tea. Like all of the grandmasters, Kobayashi Sensei was very joyful. He possessed an energy and vibrancy that made him seem much younger than his chronological age.

Instead of closing his eyes like Fukumoto Sensei did, he kept his very open and his attention focused on my teacher's every movement. Suddenly and so unexpectedly that even Tanemura Sensei was surprised; Kobayashi Sensei tried to kill my teacher! With a blinding speed and deadly accuracy, the older master unleashed a flurry of attacks. Tanemura Sensei had no recognition or understanding of what was coming his way. The angles and positions were totally unexpected and only his spiritual and "super sense" training allowed him to survive.

After Tanemura Sensei passed this test, Kobayashi Masao Sensei was finally satisfied that his new disciple had truly achieved the grandmaster level. Only after that understanding was reached, was he free to pass on Takamatsu Sensei's other secrets.

MY CONCLUSIONS

I believe that by the time my teacher met Takamatsu Sensei, the senior Master was too elderly to personally guide the young Tanemura into full maturity. Masaji Kimura Sensei, Dr. Kimbei Sato Sensei, Yoshio Fukumoto Sensei, Masao Kobayashi Sensei and Yoshiaki Hatsumi were all grandmasters of various aspects of what Takamatsu Sensei taught. They all helped to complete Tanemura Sensei's overall understanding of this deep tradition. In addition, his experiences as a patrolman and detective, martial arts student and teacher, and even as a husband, father and grandfather all combined to make Mr. Tsunehisa Tanemura Sensei the man he is today. The apprenticeships he served loyally under these five grandmasters and others combined to make Grandmaster Shoto Tanemura the incredible *budoka* that his students know and love.

AN ADVANCED BOJUTSU SWORD DISARMING TECHNIQUE

MY KYOSHI TESTING IN JAPAN

NINE DAYS THAT CHANGED MY LIFE FOREVER

Day One

THE ARRIVAL

In a big, air-conditioned car, Tanemura Sensei picked me up from Narita's new Airport. On the way to his home, we spoke to each other more freely than ever. We mostly discussed family life and Sensei seemed to be very interested in why I began training in the first place. It had been a long time since I had re-examined my motivations, and the answers didn't come out as smoothly as I had hoped. Sensei flashed a friendly smile and kept the conversation moving without seeming to notice my lack of eloquence. His good humor made the almost two-hour trip to Matsubushi Machi go quickly.

When we arrived at my apartment, my teacher promptly ordered me to get some sleep. I did what he said, mostly. But first I made a quick stop at my favorite noodle shop — the airplane food was barely edible.

Day Two

WARMING UP

It was to be my shortest trip to Japan ever. I came for one purpose, and that was to pass the *Kyoshi* (master level) spiritual awareness test. Other than a sightseeing day in the *Nikko* mountain area, most of the days and nights were spent either in the *Honbu Dojo* or my one-room apartment.

On the second day, I got to know some people from the Emerald Isle of Ireland. They were wonderful guys and played witness to much of what happened in the days to come. We all joined training that morning. It was bo-jutsu with Kotaro *Shihan*. Since the events of September 11, 2000 forced me to cancel my travel plans the year before, I hadn't seen him in two years. He was much stronger and more precise than I remembered. I believe that he is growing to be more and more like his father, though I think of him as more of a martial art older brother. Shihan ended up being my partner that day, so in addition to having my basic techniques re-corrected, I got thrown around in ways I had never experienced before.

The night session was just as intense, with an added benefit: more *Shihan* came to the *dojo*. They were practicing to participate in an *Enbu* (demonstration) at the Japan *Kobudo Tai Kai* (ancient martial arts conference) the following month. So things were a little different. Unsure of what was going to be demonstrated, everyone in the class had to be extra cautious not to get in the way of their strong techniques. For the rest of us *biken-jutsu* (secret art of the sword) was the exclusive focus of the evening. Sensei always teaches this particular subject with serious concentration.

Day Three

A NICE DISTRACTION

We drove to Nikko Futara Mountain on the third day. Tanemura Sensei explained that the area was sacred to both Shinto and Buddhist traditions. It was a wonderful time, even though the monkeys that used to greet visiting tourists had been pushed back into the forest. I know it is better for the animals to reside away from humans, but, years ago, we used to have a lot of fun feeding them. Additionally, I found it fascinating how the master recounted the way many of the practices of the shrines, temples and museums are tied to those of countries thousands of miles away. We returned without any major problems.

Day Four

MISSING IN ACTION

By 10:30 am, I had already been at the dojo for more than an hour and a half. I usually arrive for training quite early to stretch and get my head together. That morning started no different, but by later that night; something would catch up with me. Kotaro Shihan was there like clockwork, and Sensei ordered him to review my *rokudan* (sixth degree) *Jujutsu* techniques. I felt that my techniques were poor, but he was still very encouraging. When it was my turn to act as *uke* (the one who gets thrown), the younger Tanemura took me for quite a spin. He was working on several variations of the Hontai Takagi Yoshin *ryu kata*.

That evening at 8:00, I was nowhere to be found. The Irishmen knocked loudly at my door but got no response. They left for class without me, wondering why my bicycle remained locked in the rack behind the apartment. I was "dead to the world." Jet lag had finally knocked me out, though I had been trying my hardest to resist. Luckily, one of the other students happened to forget his belt and come back to the apartments. Somehow the noise rousted me as he hurriedly stormed past my door. In my groggy state, I guess I missed most of the lesson. I can't even remember what we did. Tanemura Sensei understood but warned me to be more awake for my sword test the next day.

Day Five

THE WIND OF HEAVEN COMES DOWN

It was a Saturday, so Sensei taught both classes. In the daytime, things were severe. My focus that day was Asayama Ichiden *ryu*, and boy was I messing up. I was going too fast, my center of gravity was way too high, and because I did the *waza* incorrectly, I couldn't cause enough pain to make Kotaro *Shihan* give up. Tanemura Sensei seemed about to take a little pity on me (or so I thought). At that moment, Sensei decided that the best way for me to understand it and adjust my lazy habits was to experience the techniques more fully. I can certainly say that I was in a world of pain that hour. But it worked. I had been so used to working with my passive students back home, that I had become sloppy. Between having my wrist close to being sprained and having a seasoned partner like Kotaro *Shihan*, I gained an amazing degree of clarity with those techniques.

"Turn around and wait with your eyes closed in meditation!" the Grandmaster ordered. At the end of class, Tanemura Sensei went into the weapons closet and pulled out a *fukuro-shinai* (bamboo sword, covered in white leather). I started to feel uneasy. I didn't expect Sensei to have me practice this with him that morning. "Bam!" the sword hit my shoulder. My nerves had made me a moving target.

"Be still, Michael! Relax and stop using your brain," Tanemura Sensei said directly. Suddenly there was a loud crunching sound. My nose hurt and the top of my head was numb. When I opened my eyes, there was a small cloud of suede shavings floating in the air like snowflakes. Apparently, I stayed a little too relaxed, because I was smacked so hard that the sword had bent around my forehead and hit me in the face. I told myself, "Something has got to change!"

What happened next started a chain of events that changed my life forever. My mind was completely clear. For that moment, I didn't stand out. I felt like a tree in a vast forest or a blade of grass in a rolling meadow. It was an effortless and natural state of being. The next thing I realized was that my body was traveling sideways. I heard the shinai strike the tatami. "That is the Super Sense!" my teacher said with a smile.

I was utterly speechless. I was touched by a power previously unexperienced. Tears started flowing uncontrollably, and I could offer no explanation as to why I had moved. I had attempted this test literally hundreds of times before, and I never felt anything even remotely close to this sensation. Later, Tanemura Sensei said that God had given me a great gift that day. He described the movement, "as if the wind had blown you aside on a conveyer belt." I was very grateful for this wind from Heaven, but that was only the practice session, not the real examination....

This time I decided not to tempt fate and avoided taking a nap before class. Tanemura Sensei forgave one bout of slothfulness, but a second time might have cost me this opportunity. I entered the dojo an hour early and tried my best to prepare for the exam. While I was arranging the candles on the *Kamidana,* one of the green belt students asked if something important was going to happen. I shrugged off his question and remained silent. One of his Irish roommates mercifully saved me from having to explain the source of my apprehension.

One by one, the *Honbu Dojo Shihan* arrived. Okayasu *Shihan*, Nagamoto *Shihan* and others were all in attendance. The only one I did not have the honor of having a reunion with that day was Roy Ron *Shihan*. We all exchanged bows and polite words but got down to business quickly. Sensei came in and soon we all recited the *Ninniku Seishin*. I noticed a new Amatsu Tatara patch on his back, and somehow that added to the uneasy feeling in my stomach.

All of the masters were to perform at the *Enbu* demonstration, so there was a lot of action on that side of the *dojo*. Even Sensei joined in the training, so I couldn't help but to look at his techniques. Before I knew it, class was over, and it was back to the task at hand. The *Shihan* took their place to the right of the shrine and the lower ranks crammed into one line to the left.

DOUBT LEADS TO FAILURE

Again, I was ordered to meditate. When Tanemura Sensei asked me to take my place with my back turned, I jumped up way too quickly. I was over-anxious, and he immediately told me to calm my spirit. After a while, I found myself searching for that new state of consciousness. My master was poised with a sword meant to simulate cleaving me in two. Twice before, I had failed the official test. What happened that morning was still a fresh experience, but I couldn't wrap my head around exactly how it worked.

"Pow!" was the sound of my shoulder receiving the blow. "You are guessing! Your ego is too big. Stop using your brain." Even with coaching I couldn't succeed. The Shihan seemed to understand something I couldn't, but they all remained silent. I was disappointed and confused. I strained to grasp the answer to this riddle. What did I have to do? Who did I have to be? Because who Michael Coleman was at that moment just couldn't cut it!

"Michael-san, Sensei would like to see you now. Please change clothes," Kotaro *Shihan* suddenly informed me, and I immediately straightened up.

DINNER WITH THE GRANDMASTER

The grandmaster took me to his favorite Chinese restaurant for dinner. It had been a long time since just the two of us had gone out to eat. I didn't bring my wallet to the *dojo* that night, but Sensei planned to treat me anyway. As we sipped warming tea, it was not difficult to see my inner struggle.

"You must make a choice, Michael," Tanemura Sensei began. "You have distracted yourself by dividing your focus on too many things. Other martial arts, egotistical spiritual practices, strange kinds of *Qigong*, etc. You need to make a clear decision… It is true that Takamatsu Sensei had experience studying different subjects and teachings, but in the end he chose the middle way."

"You always want to be better than everyone else and you're not," he continued resolutely. "You are just another student; just another person. No human being is superior to any other. We all just have different jobs. If you clean up your heart, you have a great mission to fulfill. But not if you are like a long nose *tengu*." (A *tengu* is a Japanese mythological, bird-man creature; the length of its nose or beak is symbolic of conceit and self-importance.)

Sensei made a motion like an inflated nose was being lopped off, and I was instantly reminded of the morning practice session. My nose was struck the first time my teacher attacked. Of course, I silently wished that I had gotten the hint then.

"You must have a serious talk with 'Michael' and find out what he wants to do with his life. You can quit *ninpo* now and continue to attain high rank in *jujutsu*. Or, you can give up your fascination and worry about rank and titles, and surrender your life to this art. This way you can discover what is the truth."

I chose to give away the petty things that I used to think were important and find out what was real.

Day Six

GIVING UP MY ROBES

I hadn't slept well the night before. With his infinite kindness, Tanemura Sensei offered to teach a private class just for the four of us. Because the lesson wasn't scheduled until the afternoon, the guys from the Emerald Isle used the opportunity to catch up on some much-needed sleep. I was fully conscious and not so lucky.

In a desperate attempt to relax, I used my laptop to listen to some music. During track 9, the computer suddenly stopped working. All computers seem to crash for no reason from time to time, so I didn't pay it much attention. I pushed the reset button, turned off the power and then finally unplugged the thing, all to no effect.

In that moment of silence, I got a strong feeling. I rose from the floor and went straight to my suitcase. I fished out the monks clothing that had been given to me by a local priest. I also gathered the prayer beads and paper that contained special mantras that had been given to me earlier. I mounted my bike and rode to the temple very quickly. When I arrived in front of his grandfather's statue, it was very cloudy. Since I had landed in Japan, it had rained, but only at night after we were all in bed. That day, the weather was beginning to change.

I walked up the stairs and looked at the five-centuries-old temple, to which I had paid my respects for over four years. I grew up Christian, but I was attracted to this particular sect of Buddhism. I had seen pictures of many martial artists doing these interesting *ketsu-in* (hand forms). I mistakenly thought that they were somehow more important than the basic *Butoku* (martial art virtues). Of course, they weren't. In addition, many of the things that lead me astray had all of the qualities I used to enjoy: they were secret, elitist and mysterious. So, they used to feed my selfish need to distance myself from other people.

For the first time, I did not bow. I stood tall and asserted my decision to follow the natural way of God. I was not angry or vindictive. I think of it now in terms of getting lost while driving. When you finally find a map, how does it help to become angry that you've been going in circles?

I descended the steps and my former sensei came to the door. He accepted my resignation with grace and told me that he understood. He was not a bad man. I just had to make a clean break. From there

I gathered my real *dogi* (uniform) and went straight to Tanemura Sensei's house.

Sensei was home but very busy. In our short conversation, I told my teacher a little of what had happened. At first, Sensei thought it all a little dramatic, but soon he acknowledged that my situation demanded more extreme measures than some. It was obvious that the Grandmaster had said all he needed about the subject, so I excused myself and let him get back to work.

TWO CHALLENGES IN THE DOJO

After what had happened the day before, I was very confused. My world had been turned upside-down. I was about two hours early, so I got dressed alone. Without any warning, my heart started racing and my breathing became irregular. My erratic thoughts made me incredibly anxious. My mind was in a vice grip. Despite my best efforts, all I could think to do was to pace and walk in circles. No change. I gripped my chest and started to breathe deeply. No change.

Finally, I sat down in seiza in front of the *Kamidana*. Without thinking, I listened to myself say silently "*Shikin Haramitsu Daikomyo*," like I had never heard it before. At once, I felt warmth and soft pressure on my forehead. The *dojo* was totally cold, but my face felt like it was in the sunshine. In my mind's eye, I looked up and saw a light shining before me. It started as a pinpoint but eventually expanded across the horizon, beyond my vision. Then another light came, from a very different place. It had a type of heat too, but the kind that I didn't want to touch. Its rays were not smooth and formed a thin crust over something dark. To think about it reminds me of a rotten piece of fruit; that looks good on the outside, but once you bite into it you can't get rid of the horrid taste in your mouth.

Everything was peaceful, and my body returned to normal. But even as I write this, I can remember the feeling very distinctly. Presently, two more students joined me in the dojo. One of them was not feeling well, and the other was a doctor. So, I listened carefully to his prognosis.

I was in the middle of listening to descriptions of various flu symptoms when Tanemura Sensei appeared at the door. He was not dressed for teaching and he had a tough-looking guy with him. I've had my share of students with rough appearances, so I didn't think twice about it. As Sensei expected, I said all the proper Japanese polite greetings. I got no response, other than some confused looks and a bit of flinching every time I moved my hands. I added, "*Hajime mashite. Dozo yoroshiku!*" which means, "Nice to meet you, please remember me!" I thrust my hand forward with a smile on my face, and the poor guy ran away. I thought it was my fault, so I was embarrassed.

Sensing my confusion, Tanemura Sensei invited me into his study and explained what had happened. The young man in his early twenties was already an experienced street fighter. He came to my teacher's home and bragged to the grandmaster about his exploits. Sensing an opportunity to put the thug in his place, Sensei invited him to a challenge match with me. In addition, Tanemura Sensei pumped up my reputation. He told the kid that I had never lost a fight and always seriously injured my opponents. Of course, I knew nothing about this contest, so I was very calm when he came to meet me. Even if I had known, compared to the inner demons I had been fighting, this guy would not have presented much of a challenge. One of the points that Sensei taught me was that people, like the one that wanted to fight, always get nervous when their adversary is too tranquil. It struck me as very funny.

Afterward, I informed my teacher of my new friends' poor health. When we went back to the dojo the rest of the guys confirmed my report. Tanemura Sensei hinted jokingly that their sickness was a side effect of what I was going through. With a doctor in our midst, he wasn't overly concerned though. On our way home, we all had a laugh about the street fighter. Even the light drizzle and impending storm didn't bother us.

Day Seven

IT TOOK AN EARTHQUAKE

The next morning, heavy rain, thunder and lightning filled the sky. There was even an earth tremor during the night. Perhaps because of the side-to-side shaking of my studio apartment, I awoke that morning with something on the forefront of my mind. I had done all the necessary calculations, but an important part of the formula was definitely missing.

To cultivate a better relationship with the Divine, my teacher has always taught us to do two things: To review regularly our thoughts, words and actions in order to learn from our mistakes and successes; and to recognize the many reasons why we should all be deeply grateful for the boundless opportunities with which we're blessed. Tanemura Sensei is never overbearing when he says these things. Soke just asks each of us to honestly examine the quality of the lives we lead.

The reflection and meditation half came very naturally, but the gratitude part was still a mystery. Then I remembered an experience I had with Sensei earlier.

"A hundred years ago, even kings couldn't have the comforts we have now," the grandmaster said when we visited Nara. We were eating traditional Japanese, sweet bean ice cream. While enjoying amazing views of mountain temples, he explained that, "Without refrigerators, the ice had to be carried from snowcapped peaks in large quantities. Of course, much of it would melt and be wasted in transit. All of this just so the *Shogun* could enjoy a cool treat in the hot sun."

The thankful heart for which I was looking was not the variety of which one normally speaks. Praying before a meal or bowing deeply at the appropriate moment are certainly good habits. However, in order to cut off my nose and lead a less egotistical life, I needed more profound insight. Finally, it came to me!

I jumped on my bike, umbrella in hand, with a refreshingly new attitude. Sheets of water were coming down and the skies were overcast. But in the core of my being, I was convinced that it was going to be a very beautiful day.

The private class was nothing short of spectacular. We all appreciated Sensei's kind attention to detail. There were only three of us that day. So, everyone had a more exclusive chance to pick up many new *kuden*. As always, the illuminating lesson seemed to end too quickly. After class, it was time to test again. But this time, I was better prepared.

Thinking logically, the idea I received seemed sound. It was based on a kind of faith that I had heretofore not possessed. But even Tanemura Sensei always acknowledges that each of his master level students has a unique personality. Over the years, for example, each of the *Shihan* have given me bits of advice. They all provided me good suggestions, but from different perspectives. Perhaps, what I imagined would work for me, but would work differently for somebody else. But I didn't have time to wonder. The moment for doubts was over. Sensei was about to test my new assumptions.

"Yoshi! Good!" my master said happily. It was finished before it had begun. It seemed that I had just sat down and forced myself to smile and "That's it!" Again Soke came at me, this time more vigorously than the first "Okay, okay," he said the third time. And by now I had a grin from ear to ear. "But next time make your *taisabaki* better, because if I were using a live blade, your feet would've been cut off." This statement made me a bit uneasy, but I stayed joyful and escaped a fourth and a fifth time, feet intact!

There was no evening class that day. So, we were free to do as we pleased. Rainy skies and fatigue stopped any plans to go into Tokyo. So, the immediate focus shifted to keeping our notes and bodies as dry as possible on the bike trip home.

Day Eight

"I WON'T LEAVE JAPAN UNTIL I PASS!"

After I made the decision to drop all affiliation with any other martial arts or religious practices, I made a vow to my Sensei. I had tickets to fly to China immediately after my stay in Japan. I told the

Grandmaster that I was willing to cancel them, and I promised not to leave the country until I had passed the *Kyoshi* exam.

Tanemura Sensei appreciated my sincerity. But as usually, I was being overly dramatic. Soke reminded me of several reasons why I actually needed to keep my plans in China. However, my resolve to complete the task at hand never wavered or got distracted by the next leg of my journey.

Way ahead of schedule, I bowed to the *Kamidana*. The sun had come out and I felt even better than the day before. There was less stress that morning, because Sensei was away from the dojo on other business. At least there would be no "decapitations" until nightfall.

I think that I was the only one that had used a razor that morning. The beard I had been growing since I landed was starting to bother me. After Tanemura Sensei described the appropriate state of mind as being like "a baby in Nature," I felt it more fitting to be clean-shaven. Sensei had directed Kotaro *Shihan* to discover what, if anything, I knew about *Rokudan* (sixth degree) *Ninpo Taijutsu*.

It'd been three years since my *Godan Ninpo Taijutsu* test; however, I didn't really know any of the sixth degree techniques. The official policy was not to teach anything above the fifth degree until this spiritual exam was successfully passed. Tanemura Sensei made no exception in my case. Everything I had seen about *Rokudan* up to then was a variation, and not the true form of the *waza*. Precautions like this are necessary to protect the integrity of the master levels.

My techniques were sketchy at best, but the young Tanemura really helped me to take many new things to heart. It was a very challenging class because, among other things, learning how to disarm a swordsman while wearing *shuko* (iron hand claws) is very complicated and potentially dangerous. I could hardly keep up with the *Shihan*. Of course, I wrote copious new notes.

THAT EVENING, THE MOMENT OF TRUTH

By seven o'clock in the evening, it was already dark. I was done with my favorite noodles and only one thing remained undone. After my customary warm-up, the dojo filled with a bunch of new people that I had never met. Greetings were exchanged and I noticed one person in particular. I'm sorry that I don't remember his name, but I know that he was Japanese and was just starting to move up the ranks. It seemed abundantly clear that being at the training hall was the most enjoyable and exciting experience he could possibly be having. I decided then and there, that he would be one of my role models. Tanemura Sensei had told me to return to the state of the "beginner's mind," and this guy really had it. When Sensei came through the door, we all stopped what we were doing and bowed. Then he asked me a simple question, "Michael, are you happy?" "Hai, Sensei!" I replied and took my place in line.

Almost two decades before, Ninpo taijutsu was the first thing that my teacher had taught me. Back then, some things were different on the outside, but the inner truths were never altered. Kotaro *Shihan* had taught me well, yet when Tanemura Sensei demonstrated the same movements; there was a spark of energy that I had never before witnessed. That night, like the first time, I was both amazed and confused by what I saw and felt. That night, under a star-filled sky, I started over again.

"We will meditate together," Tanemura Sensei said matter-of-factly. Everyone was in his appropriate spot, and this time the mood of the test felt a little different. Somehow, I knew that I would have only one chance. "*Shikin Haramitsu Daikomyo!*" we uttered in unison. Things were different this time, but I didn't allow anything to interrupt my concentration. I quietly turned around and gave my life.

Whack! The shinai hit the floor with such force that it bent almost to a ninety-degree angle. "Yoshi! (Great!) Tanemura Sensei said holding the last three letters for emphasis. I had finally passed!

My face had no tears this time, just a big stupid grin that comes back every time I think about it.

The other students congratulated me, and I took the opportunity to thank the green belt student who had been so inspirational to me. He just looked at me strangely and shook his head. I asked someone else, who's Japanese was much better than mine, to translate. After hearing a slightly better version, he kind of smiled weakly. But it was apparent that he still thought that I might have taken one too many hits to the skull.

After class, I set out alone on a country road. I pedaled to my apartment solo and very contemplatively. The sky was clear and the moon was full. The weather had definitely changed for the better, and I was going to be thankful and enjoy it.

Day Nine

DEPART BUT NEVER FORGET

In the morning, the Irish students and I took a nice trip into Tokyo. We visited a wonderful martial arts supply shop and had a variety of sweets (something I never eat at home). A couple of trains and one bus later, we were back to the apartments. I packed my luggage while the others took in another class. After I stuffed way too many things into my suitcase, I visited the Honbu Dojo one more time.

The lesson had not yet ended, so I stood motionless outside the building. I closed my eyes and listened to the familiar sounds of swords cutting the air and warriors releasing their *kiai* (spirit shouts). On the way to Matsubushi from the airport, I had told Sensei that I was glad to come alone this time, because I wanted to be just a student - free from the responsibilities of being a *dojo-cho* (teacher). After all I experienced, I realized that I was always just a student; no better or more important than any other.

Back at the *dojo*, I said my goodbyes to those with whom I had just made an acquaintance in the days prior and also to those that I had met more than a decade before. One of the *Shihans* was there too. His words were kind and understanding. Before I left he looked at me, smiled and made a newly familiar gesture with his hands. With his left hand he pulled an imaginary nose out at least four inches longer than his own. With his right hand he pretended to cut it off.

AN ADVANCED BIKENJUTSU TECHNIQUE

THE DEVELOPMENT OF THE FUTEN SHIBU

PART V

Now I am a *Shibu-cho*, Regional Director. When I started teaching, I was the lowest level instructor in the United States, today I am Tanemura Sensei's most senior representative in America. I have seen my relationship with the Grandmaster go through many evolutionary stages since the 1980's, and now he requires me to "stand up as a true *Shibu-cho*."

The next stage of development of my *Futen Shibu* is following in my teacher's footsteps. Along the way, I have ranked well over 50 instructor-level students. A good percentage of them have the skill and temperament to help others realize their basic potential in this martial art and spiritual tradition. Like the branches of a tree, a Shibu can have many *dojo* and groups. I will follow Tanemura Sensei's example and "create many satellites."

ROKUDAN

六段

"And therefore, the general who in advancing does not seek personal fame, and in withdrawing is not concerned with avoiding punishment, but whose only purpose is to protect the people and promote the best interests... is the precious jewel.... Few such are to be had."
-Sun Tzu

CHAPTER VI

KEEPING A BALANCED HEART

In Japanese, this character 忠, pronounced *"chu"* is translated as loyalty. The top radical can mean *middle, steadfast,* or *balanced* and the bottom half always refers to the *heart* or *true mind.* In my experience, I've found that certain events help to define our lives and convince us to either more seriously follow the path we are on, or choose to go a different way. This observation especially applies in regard to the relationship between a master and disciple.

Since meeting Grandmaster Shoto Tanemura in 1987, many events have told me that he is, without a doubt, the best person to teach me the true meaning and correct practice of *Bumon* and *Shumon.* Tanemura Sensei always leads by example. Indeed, I've seen Soke learning from some of his personal teachers.

Before my eyes, Tanemura Sensei has demonstrated loyalty, patience and concern for his teachers, even greater than most sons I know have shown toward their fathers. *Soke* once told me that in the old days, when a *deshi* (disciple) received the final grandmastership from his Sensei, the student was responsible for his master's well-being until death.

In 1999, I passed my examination for *Genbukan Ninpo Taijutsu Godan* (fifth-degree black belt). Three years later I earned the title of *"Kyoshi."* These two things were very significant in my life and helped to prepare me for the situation which I'm about to relate. Also, without Tanemura Sensei's guidance and experience, I surely would have fallen away from the true path of Ninpo.

LOOKING FROM THE IGA REGION TO THE KOGA REGION

MY SEARCH FOR KI

The concept of *Ki*, or internal energy, has always fascinated me. Of course, I was most delighted to hear stories of *"ku-ki-nage"* (throwing an opponent without even having to touch him). Many masters have been reported to possess such skill, but live demonstrations are hard to come by.

In the United States, the first time I asked a master of a different school to show me this power was in 1986. The result was comical. Many years later in Asia, I was given a more serious chance to truly understand more deeply. Grandmaster Tanemura asked me to include this story:

"Tanemura Sensei, perhaps I should just stay in Japan."

"No Michael," the Grandmaster said firmly. "This meeting was arranged long before you came to the Honbu Dojo. It would be bad manners for you not to show up."

"Hai, Sensei. But I want you to know that I no longer want to see this other teacher."

"I understand, Michael. Yet, I have a feeling that there is something very important that you need to learn by going to him."

"Hai, Sensei!" was all I could answer. I would soon find out what Soke meant.

THE MAINLAND

The mainland of Asia was very different than the islands of Japan. The people, the manners and the smells were all very new to me. – I even saw a street vendor shaving with an electric razor, while cooking noodles!

Though I had some experience with a few of the languages in college, there was still a barrier in communication. Yet somehow, mostly I was able to make myself understood. Thankfully, whenever I truly needed to have something translated, an English-speaking person just seemed to appear out of nowhere.

It took me two days to locate the other teacher. He was very famous in his homeland, and I'd been given several newspaper clippings that celebrated his accomplishments. Apparently, he was a national fighting champion and attributed his success to his mastery of internal energy.

At about 6:00 am, I met him and his students in a park. Every morning in that city, hundreds of martial artists and other enthusiasts choose to meet in separate parts of a large open square. This area was defined by flat concrete and the surrounding trees were ringed with thick metal spikes. Compared to the graceful *tatami* and wood walls in Matsubushi town, it was a fairly unwelcoming place.

Though the population of the city was in the tens of millions, I actually had little difficulty finding the spot. They had been expecting me, and his group seemed very friendly. I didn't know right away exactly what to say. But, after I paid the teacher, it seemed to "break the ice."

He turned to a female member of his group, twisted his hand in a strange way and did something with his eyes. Suddenly, she started to hop up and down. She just kept hopping and hopping, then looked at me and communicated that she couldn't stop herself. – After a couple of minutes of this, he simply twisted his hand again and turned her off like one would a toy.

He gave other demonstrations wherein he tossed several of his students yards away from him, simply by waving his hands. It didn't seem real. And though he may have been good at hypnotizing his disciples, I wasn't buying it. I simply smiled and thought for a moment that I had completely wasted a trip. But then, he started to demonstrate hand-to-hand fighting with his best student.

The teacher was like a snake. He seemed impossible to touch, and I could tell from my Ninpo training that he knew many dangerous pressure points. He used them frequently in his fighting style.

His student, who was larger than me, unsuccessfully tried to strike, push, and restrain his master over and over. Suddenly, after seeing him move inexplicably, a flash came to me about how to beat his style. At that moment, the teacher turned to me and asked his top fighter to go away from him and spar with me.

My Chinese wasn't advanced enough to refuse, so I quickly found myself in a face-off with his student. Instantly, I was aware of the metal spikes directly behind me. They were meant to keep animals from disturbing the trees, so I positioned myself ninety degrees to the right. His slippery arms came at my face and chest at odd angles, so I quickly dropped underneath them. With a movement I learned from KJJR Jujutsu *nidan* level, I secured his front leg. Once again, there came a strange feeling. Suddenly I knew that his next move would be to strike with his elbow to the back of my skull. To defend, I looked up to his eyes with a special *Ki* technique taught to me by Tanemura Sensei. He was somehow stunned by this and couldn't succeed with his attack. Soon after, he found himself sprawling to the hard ground.

His teacher was surprised by the outcome and ordered an immediate rematch. This time I was not allowed to go for the legs. A peaceful calm came over my body and mind. I was no longer confused. There was no fear, and I felt safe like I had donned a suit of armor.

When the opponent came at me a second time, he seemed to be moving in slow motion. My right fingertips instinctively found the middle of his chest. – *Yagyu Shingan ryu* is a style that Tanemura *Soke* first introduced me to in 1991. This was the first time I had to use it in real life. – Umpf! The heel of my palm hit him hard, but I missed his heart on purpose. He grabbed his pectoral muscle and flew back. The fight was over. Later, Tanemura Sensei told me that Sato Kimbei Sensei had used this same technique in a similar situation.

After what happened, the teacher looked at me again with different eyes. Soon, and honest smile came to the corners of his mouth. "Who is your teacher?" he asked with sincere interest. Just then, an English-speaking man came from the crowd. With his help, I was finally able to explain about my training with my only Sensei, Grandmaster Shoto Tanemura.

The next day, the other teacher asked to instruct me privately. He actually did end up showing me one real *Ki* exercise, and I felt a little bit of true energy. I recognized it because Tanemura Sensei had shown me this technique more than ten years earlier. It was only a very small part of what I was already taught. The teacher complimented me on my proper manners and good attitude. He said that he respected Tanemura Sensei a great deal and that he could see that the *Soke* was an excellent teacher.

True *Ki* does exist; we could not live without it. However, trying to control people for personal and egotistic gain can lead to very dangerous things. This fact has been proven many times. Tanemura Sensei taught me that the best *Ki* training is naturally achieved by studying our Amatsu Tatara arts. Correct understanding and use of *Ki* should lead to three things: better techniques, more health and greater happiness. If these qualities are not experienced, one is training incorrectly.

BEYOND KYOSHI

After I left Japan, I quickly realized that passing the *Kyoshi* test was by no means the end of my training. The touch of spirit I felt helped to renew my faith that all of this punching and kicking would ultimately lead to some higher understanding. Yet, it was clearly up to me whether I used my skills to help other people or feed my own ego.

Having Tanemura Sensei as my role model was then and is now the key to my success. The Chinese and Japanese character 師, pronounced *"shi"* is translated as "master," but its deeper meaning is "a person worthy of emulating." Of course, a true master serves as a positive role model. If that teacher allows his heart to become dark, he is no longer worthy of the title.

Without a morally enlightened example and a student who is sincere, knowing how to stay on the middle path is challenging. Without mutual trust and loyalty, it is impossible to get close to the master. And, without that intimate relationship, there can be no depth of teaching and understanding.

Soke says, most of the lessons learned after the "master level" are imparted without words. These empirical experiences can sometimes trigger surprisingly strong emotions; and I believe this is because of the depth of spiritual connection between teacher and disciple.

SOKE IN MEDITATION

TANEMURA SENSEI FLOWS EFFORTLESSLY FROM *ONIKUDAKI*

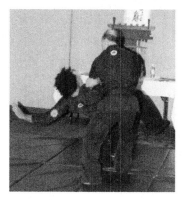

TABLE MANNERS

A few of my students and I walked into a Japanese restaurant. As is the custom, I wrote my name down along with the number of people in my party and we waited patiently in the reception area for my name to be called. A few minutes later, about twenty students from a different martial arts organization entered the same restaurant. Without a pause, they spread out across the dining area. They sat down wherever they pleased in groups of three or four; some even went so far as to pour themselves coffee without saying anything to anybody.

As politely as he could, the restaurant manager went over to each table and tried to explain the proper manners. He gestured over to my group and a few other patrons that had arrived before them. Their leader shot an agitated glance at the relatively short line ahead of them. Impatiently he announced to his entire group that they were all to leave immediately. His students filed out in front of mine saying rude things under their breath. A few even left half-full glasses at the drink bar.

I told this story to Grandmaster Tanemura while eating lunch with him in *Koshigaya*. He asked me to include it in this book and instructed me further in the art of Japanese table manners.

ROKUDAN TRAINING

In the winter of 2002, I received my *rokudan* (6th degree black belt) in KJJR Jujutsu. It was very significant to me because before then, I could never really imagine achieving any level beyond *godan*. Of course, when I was in Japan I had taken break-falls for even higher level students of the grandmaster; but it is a different thing to put yourself in their shoes.

As I had previously written, my *ninpo rokudan* training started years before. But as I progressed, Tanemura Sensei taught deeper *kuden* and each time I felt as if I were starting anew. These revelations forever changed my understanding of what it meant to be *rokudan*. Loyalty and steadfastness are the main components necessary to survive after this level.

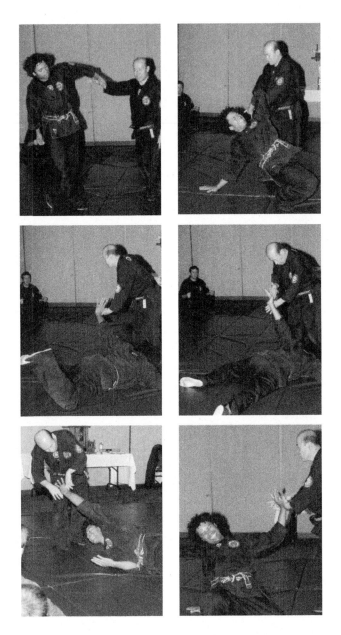

1.

THE GRANDMASTER CONTROLS THE AUTHOR'S
BODY WITH HIS TAISABAKI AND KI

THE NEW HONBU DOJO

Even at 8:00 in the morning, the Honbu Dojo was very hot. The thermometer read 37° Celsius with no promise of it going any lower.

After an hour, Tanemura Sensei appeared at the door. I had just finished reviewing my *ninpo taijutsu* techniques on my own; and though I had left my *gi* top folded in the corner, my shirt and pants were completely wet.

"Michael, come and see the new Honbu Dojo," Tanemura Sensei said with a big smile.

I happily bowed to the *kamidana*, slipped into my sandals, and followed the grandmaster.

Carpenters and contractors were already busy at work. Outside they were cutting ceramic tiles; and inside. They were applying finishing touches with wood and metal.

A CARPENTER HARD AT WORK

With the skill and pride of a tour guide, Tanemura Sensei led me through the spectacular new rooms. The new *kamidana* had a beautiful frame of exotic, dark timbers. The main offices had a special window from which the Grandmaster could spy on the dojo activities.

"Here you can make omelets for breakfast," Tanemura *Soke* remarked as he pointed out the kitchen just off the main hallway.

Dressing rooms, showers, and VIP viewing areas were never part of the old dojo, but now Tanemura Sensei's dream had come true.

"YOU WOULD BE DEAD."

As we came down the stairs from the second floor, Tanemura Sensei explained how busy his morning was going to be. Kotaro *Shihan* was going to be my teacher for the first class, and I was happy to work with him again.

In Japan, the main difference with this kind of training was that the *shihan* would both teach me my techniques and perform his techniques on me. Because Kotaro *Shihan* is my senior, I always get to experience very advanced and (sometimes) frightening new *waza*.

"Michael, please sit or else you will knock down (go unconscious)," Kotaro *Shihan* ordered in all seriousness.

It took me a second to understand what he meant, but I was very clearly suffering the effects of the heat and humidity. Even with water, I couldn't seem to cool down. The heat seemed to radiate out from my body and into my face at the same time. Thankfully, I was able to survive until the class ended at noon.

Later that evening, Tanemura Sensei was the teacher. Soke had just finished correcting every one of my *Ninpo rokudan* techniques, and I realized that I had never seen some of the modified stances before. But he explained that they were the original postures and were rarely revealed to the public.

"You would be dead!" the Grandmaster pointed out after I had poorly executed a *muto-dori* (sword- disarming) technique.

"Kotaro *Shihan*, get a *shinai* (bamboo sword). Michael, I will be your attacker," Tanemura Sensei went on to say.

"BAM!" was the familiar sound of bamboo striking the top of my head. I had squared off with the Grandmaster, and tried to execute the *kata*. Then, Tanemura Sensei handed me the sword. His calmness was very unnerving, but with all the courage I could muster, I launched my strike.

The next thing I knew, three fingers found their mark outside of my throat, and a half-second later, there was a sharp pain in my ribs. I guess it's strange to say that as I fell there was a smile on my face.

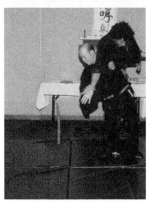

TANEMURA SOKE DOING A SHORT SWORD DISARMING
TECHNIQUE (NOTICE HOW THE SWORD BOUNCES OFF
THE FLOOR & HOW HE AUTOMATICALLY ESCAPES)

"In the *Amatsu Tatara* scrolls it is written how to defeat a swordsman. However, your defense was incorrect and impatient, and the attacker could clearly see your intentions. I used a secret theory. So even though you have done this technique many times, you could not understand my defense. Now I will teach you how to stay alive."

TENSHIN HYOHO KUKISHIN RYU BOJUTSU

In the first year of the Engen era (1336) on August, 28th, Yakushimaru Kurando Takamasa, who was the 37th generation from a famous bloodline starting with Fujiwara Kamatari, helped Emporer Godaigo escape from Kazan palace. The Emporer had been trapped at Kazan by shogun Ashikaga Takauji. To gain entrance, Takamasa dressed as a woman, taking with him a traditional woman's weapon, the *naginata*, so that the guards let him pass. However, he was discovered escaping with the Emporer and he had to fight Satake Goromaru Takenobu, a retainer of Ashikaga Takauji.

Goromaru cut the blade end off Takamasa's naginata, but Takamasa used the metal bands on the bottom end of the remaining *rokushakubo*, to strike a deadly blow to

Goromaru's head. He then fought the rest of Takauji's guards, still using only his *rokushakubo* and in the end was successful. In December of the second year of the Engen era (1337), Takamasa was given the family name Kuki (Kukami) by Emperor Godaigo, for his loyalty and successful rescue mission. After that, Takamasa gave more credence to *rokushaku bojutsu* in his martial art Tenshin Hyoho Kukishin ryu.

On May 4th of the 3rd year of the Tensho Era (1534), daimyo Takeda Katsuyori's army fought against the combined forces of daimyo Oda Nobunaga and daimyo Tokugawa Ieyasu, at Narashino, Aichi prefecture. During this battle, Takeda's retainer, Suzuki Tango Katsuhisa, fought with Kuriyama Ukon Nagafusa. Kuriyama attacked Suzuki with his *yari*, but Suzuki countered with his tachi and cut the *yari* in two. Using the remaining *sanjaku bo* (*hanbo*), Kuriyama struck and killed Suzuki. After this encounter, Kuriyama raised the importance of sanjaku bojutsu training within Tenshin Hyoho Kukishin ryu, as previously it had only included rokushaku bo.

Takamatsu Toshitsugu gave this *ryuha* (*menkyo kaiden*) to one of his highest students, Kimura Masaji. Kimura Masaji gave menkyo kaiden grandmastership and Souden-no-maki (final teachings scroll) to Tanemura Shoto, on November 10th, 1991. The genealogy is as follows:

Yakushimaru Kurando Takamasa - Ohuchi Minbu Yoshikane - Ohuchi Goromaru Katsushige - Hataketama Saburohyoe Masayoshi - Ohkuni Kawachinokami Yoshiie - Ohkuni Onihei Hisayoshi - Arima Daisuke Tadaaki - Arima Kawachinosuke Masayoshi - Kuriyana Ukon Nagafusa - Hosoya Shinpachiro Yukihisa - Kimura Ittosai Josui - Kimura Yoshinari Gessui - Ohkuma Shima Masanobu - Iba Toyotaro - Ishitani Matsutaro Tadaaki - Takamatsu Toshitsugu Kikaku - Kimura Masaji Masakatsu - Tanemura Tsunehisa Shoto.

~Tanemura Shoto Sensei

HONTAI KUKISHIN RYU BO-JUTSU

Hontai Kukishin Ryu Bojutsu developed from Takagi Ryu Bojutsu. From the first grandmaster, Takagi Oriemon until the 3rd generation grandmaster, Takagi Gennoshin, it was taught as Takagi Ryu Rojutsu. Then Takagi Gennoshin tested his skills against Ohkuni Onihei, the Kukishin Ryu grandmaster. Takagi was the superior *jujutsu* warrior, but his *bojutsu* was inferior, so he awarded Ohkuni the 4th generation grandmastership. Ohkuni founded the Hontai Kukishin Ryu *bojutsu* system and Hontai Takagi Yoshin Ryu *jujutsu* system from these schools. Therefore, the true Hontai Takagi Yoshin Ryu *jujutsu* grandmaster must also have *menkyo kaiden* in Hontai Kukishin Ryu bojutsu, as these two schools and *densho* (secret books), cannot be separated. Further proof is that the true grandmaster will also have received secret bojutsu techniques and *kyusho* (healing points) documents. Takamatsu Toshitsugu gave this grandmastership to Sato Kimbei Sensei in May 1952. In turn, Sato Kimbei Sensei passed it on to Tanemura Shoto Soke in October 1989.

Grandmaster genealogy: Takagi Oriemon – Takagi Umanosuke – Takagi Gennoshin – Ohkuni Onihei – Ohkuni Yakuro – Ohkuni Tarodayu – Ohkuni Kihyoe –

Ohkuni Yozaemon – Nakayama Jinnai – Ohkuni Buemon – Nakayama Kazaemon – Ohkuni Kamaji – Yagi Ikugoro – Ishitani Takema – Ishitani Matsutaro – Takamatsu Toshitsugu – Sato Kimbei – Tanemura Shoto.

~ Tanemua Shoto Sensei

MANY GRANDMASTERSHIPS

Every time I see a list of Tanemura Sensei's grandmasterships, I am amazed at the sheer volume of family traditions that have been entrusted to Soke. Now that I've trained with him for most of my life, I can see clearly why these secrets were given to my teacher for safekeeping. Tanemura Sensei never loses sight of the goal of martial arts, and he understands completely that his purpose as headmaster is to inspire virtue and instill confidence in his disciples. I feel truly honored to be his student. Even if Sensei only taught one *ryuha*.

HURRICANE EXPERIENCE PART I – KUJIKIRI IN AMERICA

For years I had heard stories of the ninja's magical powers. *Kujikiri* (spiritual sword cutting) was one of the most intriguing subjects. By simply concentrating his mind, folding his fingers into a special position, and tracing cuts through the air the ninja were reported to evoke incredible powers. Influencing other's minds and parting clouds were just a few of the magical abilities written about.

TANEMURA SENSEI STARTING WITH KUJI KIRI

The following story could be interpreted a number of ways. Some people would call it luck, or a happy coincidence, others, Divine Providence. But, no matter what your belief, I can assure you that everything written is the truth.

I was on a vacation in New Orleans some years ago. An extremely powerful hurricane was poised to strike the next day. The city was built underneath sea level, so a direct hit—which was predicted—would break the levies and flood the streets. Many of the stores' windows had been boarded up. As an additional precaution, sandbags had been stacked outside of people's front doors. In an attempt to flee the coming devastation, the expressway was clogged with people frantically trying to find higher ground.

I had no luck renting a car, so I found myself sequestered in a ground-level hotel room in the French Quarter. The restaurants had run out of much of their food because no delivery trucks would enter the city. Thousands of people were relocated to the "Superdome" sports stadium because their poorly constructed homes would be no match for the high-velocity winds.

The night before the storm was about to hit, I called Tanemura Sensei in Japan. He had no idea that I was in harm's way, but I quickly explained the situation. I don't know what I expected him to do so many thousands of miles away, but somehow it felt better just to reach out to Soke.

"Michael, you must do a *kujikiri* prayer," Sensei said after a few moments of consideration.

"Sensei, I don't know how to do *kujikiri* against a hurricane."

"You know very well what to do, Michael. Just open your heart and stay true to what I have taught you. Here in Japan, I will also do *kujikiri* to help you and the other people. Together we will combine our best efforts."

When I woke up the next day, I was very surprised to see that the skies were completely clear. The sun shone brightly on the now nearly deserted city. Some time in the evening, the storm had taken a sharp right turn towards the North and the city was spared!

NANADAN

"Speed in the martial arts is not the True Way. Concerning
speed, we say that something is fast or slow depending
on whether it misses the proper rhythm of things."
~ Miyamoto Musashi

CHAPTER VII

EXPERIENCE PART II –
NOAH'S ARK IN JAPAN

Along with a group from Mexico and another from Ireland, my six renshi-level students and I were among the first to stay in the newly built "Genbukan House." Completed just a month before we moved in, the Genbukan house had all the latest technological advances that Japan could offer. With a maximum capacity of twenty people, it could easily accommodate all three of our small groups. We at no time felt claustrophobic.

The next few weeks provided a whirlwind of activities: hard training and testing, cleaning and reflection, and the most unbelievable weather patterns I've ever experienced.

On the first day of training, the sun beat down with a vengeance. I even bought a new umbrella to shield me from its blazing intensity. That part of Japan does not frequently experience 85°F/30°C in October. But this was not going to be a usual October.

As the group collected their luggage from the airport van, we all marveled at the glimmering, new residence. It was my twenty-sixth time training at the Honbu dojo, yet this experience was novel and unfamiliar. The massive front door had two strong security locks. Even so, after removing my shoes and tiptoeing into the main living space, the interior still felt warm and inviting.

The first order of business was to tour the facility and learn about the proper use of each button, switch, knob, latch and appliance. After the kitchen spaces were properly divvied up for food preparation and storage, the next order of business was to pick the sleeping arrangements. I was given the responsibility to oversee the entire house, which included the duties of choosing which of the five bedrooms belonged to whom.

In regard to the Honbu dojo training, I knew the schedule and sequence of events by heart. The first day was always spent recovering from the effects of our long airline flights. The next two days would include intense morning and evening training sessions. The fourth day, a gentler practice like Chinese martial arts was the norm. And the following day, we were allowed another respite before stepping up to the challenge all over again.

However, even on "rest days," the Honbu Dojo was temptingly available for self-training. And since most of the inhabitants of the house had the habit of studying martial arts for over twenty years, each of us couldn't help but opt for the extra practice. This went on smoothly for the first week. But in the second week, the weather shook things up dramatically.

A BIG STORM WAS BREWING

"Classes will be cancelled on Saturday." Tanemura Sensei said gravely. As the Grandmaster related the facts, I couldn't help but be reminded of the hurricane I had experienced in New Orleans years before. But from what Soke related, this typhoon (hurricane) promised to be even more powerful.

It was fortunate that Tanemura Sensei warned us to prepare several days before. Because, closer to the storm, the stores had completely run out of water, noodles and other basic necessities. People were starting to feel the stress and anxiety that unfortunately comes with an event of this magnitude.

Starting in the evening, the following events all happened within a 24-hour period.

First, there was a tornado that spun out ahead of the storm at sea and made landfall on its own accord. Next came the outer arms of the hurricane. The clouds were triple the height of a normal typhoon which made it a category five hurricane. Enormous amounts of rain pounded the countryside, and the wind rattled even the double-reinforced windows of our dwelling.

I was sitting atop my bed in the thick of it, and incredibly, the ground and walls began to shake and sway. Dorothy's experience in the "Wizard of Oz" came to mind, and I thought, "If these gale-force winds are actually strong enough to lift this house, we are really in trouble!"

It turned out that, in fact, what I felt was a significant earth tremor that hit precisely at that moment. After a few minutes, I realized as much, and switched my focus to taking care of the other people in the house. Further support came when Tanemura Sensei called to check on everyone in the Genbukan House. As I gave my report, I naturally forgot about my own trepidation and concentrated on keeping the other members as free from worry as possible.

Part of the preparations included moving everyone who was sleeping down on the first floor and cramming them together up on the second level. We were also told to sleep in our clothes, so if we had to evacuate, we could save time. These precautions were absolutely necessary.

Tanemura Sensei had taught me that floods can be eerily silent killers. During the night when the victim is sleeping, large amounts of dark water can seep into the home noiselessly. By the time the person in question regains consciousness, it is already too late. The room will most likely be filled with water up to their nose and the unfortunate sleeper oftentimes drowns in their bed.

Being sequestered together in such close quarters immediately brought to mind being stuck on a ship at sea. The Grandmaster and I both used the same nautical metaphor, and Tanemura Sensei recalled the biblical story of Noah and the Ark. If Soke was Noah, then we were his sons. And collectively, we literally embodied hundreds of years of studying this martial art with Soke. Instead of the DNA of animals, the genetic code we protected was born of our individual decades of training in Tanemura Sensei's *ryuha* (martial art traditions). But the most dangerous part of the flood didn't reveal itself until the next day.

I greeted the sunrise alone. I woke up solo around 4:30 am. I descended carefully down the stairs, and thankfully the first level was as dry as it was the day before. After pulling up the metal shades, the sun shone so bright it hurt my eyes. However, the clear skies and beautiful sunrise were misleading. At that time, I didn't know that the middle river that lay between Tanemura Sensei's house and ours had already flooded over and blocked some roads.

Appreciatively, we were in a relatively rural Japanese area where rice paddies still existed. These carefully dug trenches and rows of plants had been cultivated for centuries. The ancient irrigation system was ready-made to receive the excess water. Thank God, the Honbu Dojo was spared any noticeable damage.

After getting a call from Tanemura Sensei, I was finally allowed to venture out of the house for the first time in more than a day. The first thing I did was go to the bridge at the top of the hill. Directly above the house was a much larger river called the Edogawa. In the old days, there used to be a golf course next to the riverbed.

That morning, my mouth fell wide open. I was amazed to see that the level had risen so many meters that the rushing torrent seemed within reach. Fast-moving, mocha-colored rainwater completely washed over and covered up where the golf course used to be. I could hardly remember the direction of the bike path and running trails which now lay under incalculable gallons of water gathering flood strength and getting higher by the minute.

Several of my other students joined me in witnessing this phenomenon. We all realized that if the water reached the top of the banks, the house was in the greatest danger yet. Uncertain hours passed, but thankfully the waters eventually receded, and things returned relatively to normal.

Unfortunately, not everyone in Japan was as lucky as we were. More than fifty people were either found dead or are still missing after this natural disaster. Our deepest condolences to the families of those unfortunate souls.

TANEMURA SENSEI AT 19 YEARS OF AGE

More than a decade before this book was written, I was training in the Genbukan Honbu Dojo in Japan for several weeks, as I do each year. – It was a warm summer night. And, many master-level Shihan students were there too. Okayasu Shihan, Nagamoto Shihan, Roy Ron Shihan, Kohtaroh Shihan and Nicola Shihan were all in attendance. That evening, the Grandmaster was teaching *Naginata-jutsu* (Japanese halberd techniques). – Yet for me, what happened after we bowed out of class made it an even more special evening.

The list that follows is taken from my notes about what Tanemura Sensei shared that night. Soke copied these notes down from the writings of Toda Shinryuken Masamitsu Sensei (one of Takamatsu Sensei's teachers) when Soke was only 19 years old in 1966.

武風 Bufu (Martial Arts Wind)

A true Bushi (warrior) has God's righteousness
(神の義理)
- Is a true gentleman
- Is reserved and steps back all the time
- Shows mercy and love easily
- Never gossips or tells bad stories
- Is grateful
- Is kind and gentle
- Trains hard and is prepared to do defense in a true case
- Can stop a violent person and knows how
  to safely help weaker people
- Can smile in difficult times and does not hold on to grudges
- Has inner patience and wants never to draw a sword
- Keeps a steady heart (fudoshin)

- Has developed Kajo Waraku (the flower heart)
  and Kajo Chikusei (the bamboo heart)
- Never fights EXPLAIN LATER IN THIS CHAPTER
- Learns many things about culture and martial arts
"With Bufu Ikkan we can attain Shin Shin, Shin
Gan (God's Heart/Mind, God's Eyes/Vision)!"

THIS WAS WRITTEN THE DAY I MET
SENSEI WHEN I WAS 19 YEARS OLD

NOTES FROM SOKE'S LECTURES

My goal is for this chapter of the book to contain as few of *my* words as possible.

I am a witness to my teacher's wisdom. And, by the time that this book is published, I will have been following Soke, for over 30 years.

The permission given to Soke in 1966 was very rare. In the old days, students were not permitted to take notes or even ask questions. We were all supposed to keep the teachings only in our hearts.

This precaution undoubtedly helped to guard against people stealing our secret techniques in the past. But, Tanemura Sensei lifted that rule, and I'm very glad that Soke did.

The Grandmaster has often said that true communication and teaching will always be heart-to-heart (*i-shin den-shin*). So it is that there are many teachings in our tradition that are still transmitted only in the ancient, *kuden* way.

Even so, when Tanemura Sensei told me stories about being a much younger man, Soke sometimes referred to himself as "Question Boy." I could imagine myself also being called that name.

Tanemura Soke remembers well the difficult feeling of being unsure, but not being permitted to ask for clarification. Also, Sensei realized the value of retaining the details and *kuden* learned from the masters, especially in order to preserve the original transmissions for the next generation.

For me...without these changes, capturing hundreds of points from Soke's lectures since the 1980's would've been simply impossible.

"MICHAEL, WRITE A NEW BOOK"

Months before my seventh degree ninpo taijutsu test, Tanemura Sensei made a request. "Michael, write a book based on your notes from my lectures." It will also be translated into Spanish.

"Hai, Sensei. It will be finished within six months."

Following are some of the main points from that manuscript, organized into eight parts. Each part denotes one aspect of living a correct life. In addition, I include an essay that Soke wrote soon after I first met the Grandmaster. I felt it was a fitting and poetic way to introduce these eternal teachings.

PART 1

正見

SHOKEN - CORRECT SEEING

Spring has come and already many flowers have bloomed and gone. The spring winds are quickly blowing in[to] the summer. Like this, the shinobi no mono (true ninja), being you and I, must have the ability to keep pace with the change in seasons in the world around us.

* Bufu "Kancho's Greetings – April 1989

I

この界
あの界

Life is forever, we never die. However, everyone will for sure experience death in **this world** (the physical world). So, every second we are here before we graduate into **that world** (the spiritual world) is very precious, too. Even just minutes before a person dies, they can realize something very important that can help them in the next world.

During lessons from your teachers, listen deeply and learn at least one new thing each time. Each day you live, be sure to take a few moments to reflect about them!

* Japan Honbu Dojo Training, October 2014

II

中道

Chudo **is the center way.** We should not seek the extremes of too much pleasure or too much pain. Heaven wants us to live balanced lives.

Bringing the hands together in prayer position, called *gassho*, **is symbolic of our wish to follow the middle way,** *chudo*. Remember this when you pray daily. Correct seeing is important. Not only one side, but rather we need to view BOTH sides. If only one side you can't understand the depth or reach correctly.

* Japan Taikai, October 2015 and Japan Honbu, February 2008

III

忍耐精神

These are two enlightenment points of *Nintai Seishin*:
1) Absolute patience
2) The ability to bear even the greatest shame without resentment
Be humble and remember that all humans make mistakes. Do not allow shame and fear to cripple your heart. - Everyday practice using fudoshin to beat anger, jealousy and grudges.

* Japan Honbu Dojo Instructor Training, December 2006

PART 2

正話

SHOGO - CORRECT SPEAKING

There always exist the traditional ideas but affected by transformations with new inspirations. In this world, change is an inevitable force. Everything is affected. All things are born, raised, developed and passed on. This is how it should be in the proper scheme of things.

* Bufu "Kancho's Greetings – April, 1989

I

言霊

Be careful and always watch the words you say. Start by using positive, good manner words. Also, as a martial artist, learn to pronounce all of your Japanese technique names correctly, etc. In any language it is the same… If you change the pronunciation, you change the meaning.

Kotodama **(word soul) are the spiritual vibratory waves contained in the syllables of words.** Two important examples are "Ah", when we are born (opening) and "Un", when we pass away (closing). Everyday words have power too. This has been proven by science many times. These affect the body, mind and subconscious. Also, there are special words that can issue light-energy.

* Japan Honbu Dojo Japan Instructor Training, December 2006 and Japan Honbu Training, November 2015

II
花情竹性

Proper manners include showing respect and loyalty to your teachers and elders. In addition to being individually important, it's an especially significant lesson for the next generation to learn.

This quality should develop naturally. However, if it doesn't, there can be dire consequences. For example, when one becomes egotistical, they usually show disrespect to their personal teacher. They might even abandon a true master after they've stolen some of the secrets of his authentic lineage.

But of course, this person will find no solace. It is obviously not the correct way. And worse, his students will follow in his footsteps, eventually betraying him with the same lack of respect.

At the beginner level, the easiest way to show respect and avoid trouble is to simply follow the rules. Remember that each rule was written for a very good reason. At the master level more devotion is necessary in order to be trusted with the higher secrets.

* Japan Honbu Training, July 2010 and Japan Taikai, October 2015

III

花情和楽

Kajo waraku **is the «flower heart» that can enjoy peace and experience contentment.**

Have a heart that is gentle and patient, do not become aggressive in difficult situations. Keep training throughout life and study *nintai seishin* also.

Kajo Chikusei **is the «bamboo heart» personality that can endure even strong winds.**

Develop a heart that is strong and straight like a *bo* (six-foot staff), but also flexible. Keep training and study *fudoshin* also.

* Japan Honbu Dojo Instructor Training, December 2006

PART 3

正思

SHOSHI - CORRECT THINKING

There is the power of nature in its ability to flexibly adapt. We must have and experience such power in the course of our daily lives and practices. But however, much we adapt and change with the circumstances, the deep heart must remain unmoved. The heart following the purpose of *Shin Shin Shin Gan* (God's eyes and God's heart) keeps *Fudoshin* (indomitable spirit). * Bufu "Kancho's Greetings – April, 1989

I

The conscious and the subconscious are like an iceberg, only 10% is conscious and 90% is unconscious in most human beings. - *Shin shin shiki o shinobu* (from the *Ninniku Seishin*) means that we must have fortitude and constantly train the body, mind and subconscious.

In any state of consciousness, our physical reality is a "test world". Each day we must do our best to follow *chudo* (the middle way) in how we act physically, mentally and even in our dreams!

* USA Milwaukee Taikai, July 2006

II

Thinking is a direct result of what is seen and heard, and it is only afterwards that we act. There exists a cause and effect for each and every action. Jesus Christ taught us: If you do a bad thing in your mind, already you did an action!

Each day apologize sincerely from the heart for your bad thoughts. Try to look at difficult situations from the point of view of another.

* Japan Taikai Instructor Training, October 2007
and Japan Honbu Interview, February 2008

III

正直

There are three main traits of a true ninja: The first is honesty. It applies to everything. It is the «pure mirror heart» that yields correct judgment and Heaven›s equanimity.

The way of truth is the hard way! Accept this and be consistently honest with other people and yourself.

PART 4

正業

SHOGYO - CORRECT WORKING

So it is that whatever happens in life is in keeping with the decision of Heaven. The judgment of God governs all events. This frees us from reacting to outside provocations with anger, frustration, betrayal, or sadness. We can relax and continue on our way knowing all to be in the hands of the cosmic. This is the truth of Shin Shin Shin Gan. So then following the way of nature, all is brightened, and we become enchanted with the light.

* Bufu "Kancho's Greetings – April, 1989

I

As humans, we have five fingers. These can correspond to the five elements [*chi, sui, ka, fu* and *ku*]. Therefore we, like the Creator, have the power make something in this world also. Our work throughout life, even small things, is our contribution to help make the world better.

Your business or work should be helping other people as much as possible. Correct work is a SERVICE vocation not a business that takes advantage of others. This is a true job and an example of what is meant by correct working.

* Japan Taikai, October 2012 and Japan
Honbu Interview, February 2008

II

人生の波

I have said this many times...

Life has up and down waves. We must have gratitude for any level of employment or situation. You do not have to be rich to find real happiness.

My father's bloodline is connected to the emperor of Japan. For that and other reasons, our family enjoyed many privileges and high social status before WWII. However, most of that was lost during the war. So, my father had to step down and become a farmer at 45 years old. At that time, our family could not even afford to buy rice... during those difficult times we survived on potatoes.

The most difficult kind of patience to endure is when you are hungry and have no food.

During up (easy) times, don't be overly happy. Save some of your extra money, etc., so that during down (challenging) times, you can be prepared to survive. Also, do not gamble. You can find another way to make the money you need and survive.

* Japan Taikai, October 2005 and Japan
Honbu Dojo, February 2008

III

雇用主
=
従業員

In *shogyo* (correct working), the employer and employee should be viewed as equal. Each position has its proper place and responsibilities. The company should be like a family, similar to parents and children. Like children, employees should show as much support for the parent company as possible. And in turn, the management should support them accordingly. So, of course everyone needs to receive money in order to survive. BOTH should profit harmoniously.

Wherever you are employed, do your best to create and maintain a positive work environment. Attend to your responsibilities honestly and sincerely. Use virtuous actions and good character to naturally progress. Do not use schemes, rumors or lies.

* Japan Honbu Dojo Training, February 2008

PART 5

正命

SHOMYO - CORRECT LIVING

Having *fudoshin*, one attains a powerful mind. Keeping this heart, one can reach a natural happiness without additional effort or friction. In order to create *fudoshin* in the heart, don't let yourself be misled by any negative emotions. Strive [toward], reach for, and believe in the great natural way. In as much as you are able, do your best in all actions and situations.

* Bufu "Kancho's Greetings – April, 1989

I

Why do we have to spend a life as a human being? The answer is that we came to this world for training. This is so that we can grade up our souls and correct our karma. *Sei* means "life" and *myo* means "order" [how it is arranged]. This chance is also a gift from God.

We do not have very much time on earth, and we can pass away any day. Correct your mistakes as soon as possible. Don't waste your life!

* Japan Honbu Dojo Training, April 2012

人生
の
目的

II

因縁運命

All living things have fate and destiny. Everything that is born is experiencing training and must eventually die. But, the spiritual quality of any life can be graded-up for sure.

Especially in the face of adversity, don't allow yourself to be over-disappointed! You will make progress step-by-step. Keep going with the correct heart, sincere effort and relentless patience.

* USA Milwaukee Taikai, July 2003

正心 = 中道

What is the correct heart throughout your life? It is "chudo" (the middle way)! This is simple to express in words, but more difficult to stick to in actions.

A baby is born from the center of its mother... From childhood until we die, we must learn to follow the center way in all things!

* Japan Taikai, October 2015

III

習慣

Any misfortune or bad habits can indeed be conquered by you. The source of the problem lies within oneself and so does the power to correct your lack points.

Be encouraged! Circumstances can always be made more tolerable. If you honestly wish to become a better person, you can be.

* Japan Honbu Dojo Instructor Training, December 2006

PART 6

正進

SHOSHIN - CORRECT WAY

The Gods in heaven will take care of you. Be grateful to them. As completely as you're able, accomplish your life's work and mission. Always I say these things to you. This is the purpose of your being in this world. It is for us to upgrade our souls and do a mission. We are not here to play.

* Bufu "Kancho's Greetings – April, 1989

I

As I've told you before, the most important things are spirit, mind and heart. So how does one judge or measure the correct way? Start by understanding these three:

- By using correct seeing, we endeavor to perceive rightly. So, we were given two eyes...

- We also need correct hearing and listening. So, we were given two ears...

- Of course, we require correct speaking, too. So, Heaven gave us only one mouth! – We should never have two tongues like a snake. Instead, we must speak the truth exclusively.

* Japan Honbu Dojo Instructor Training 2006 and
Japan Honbu Dojo Interview, February 2008

II

幸福

We must find happiness in this very moment! In doing so, we have to also remember to keep control of our desires. If unchecked, selfish wants can grow to become insatiable.

Consider how fortunate you are already. For example: Do you already have a place to live and food each day?

Many people don't even have these basic necessities. Of course, we should be grateful for the simplest conveniences. From this basic foundation, we can start to build true happiness step-by-step. This approach can also help avoid being misled by the allure of false prosperity.

No one knows exactly the moment they will die. So, it's imperative to stay on the correct path and do your best every single day.

Also, remember not to hold onto resentment or regret about what you could not do in the past. Instead, concentrate on what you can do and the next step directly in front of you.

* Japan Honbu Dojo, February 2008

III

宿業

What is karma?

Karma is egoism, selfishness and harmful habits. For example, if someone over-drinks alcohol to the point that they're continually violent, that is showing "alcohol-karma" and other negative traits.

Throughout your entire life, use the *hansei* (reflection) that I teach to discover and root out the source of your karmic lack points. Daily application of this theory and technique will certainly help to lessen the exhausting effects of the hills and valleys which inevitably arise on the road of life. From the viewpoint of efficiency, it's always better to do this a little at a time than to wait for years and try to remove a mountain of bad habits.

* Japan Honbu Dojo Instructor Training, December 2006

行く先先宮です

Everywhere can be a shrine.

With the proper training, it is possible to rediscover the correct path from any place at any time.

* Japan Honbu Dojo Instructor Training, December 2006 and Japan Honbu Training, April 2012

行く先先道場です

Everywhere is a dojo.

We are constantly doing _shingyo_ (spiritual training) on our life path. Therefore, any place we are standing can be used to train our soul. This applies even during our dreams.

* Japan Honbu Dojo Instructor Training, December 2006 and Japan Taikai, October 2015

PART 7

正念

SHONEN - CORRECT PRAYING

The severity and hardships of life are normal and expected things. The causes of suffering are six: eyes, ears, mouth, nose, skin and mind. These lead to our downfall. But, if they are controlled by the brakes and steering wheel of the proper heart, their effects can be reversed to give us a life of paradise.

* Bufu "Kancho's Greetings – April 1989

I

Shonen **is how to pray in the correct way.** *Sho* is correct. *Nen* means mind power. So, how does one use proper mental power?

The answer to this is very important for everyone to understand: martial artists, priests and everyday people. If you can master this *shonen* you can develop a special ability to maintain happiness even in difficult times...

実は何でか？

The key to approaching shonen correctly is to constantly remember what is the truth. By vigilant self-reflection, it is possible to understand deeply what things are correct and what things are wrong.

Keep questioning, questioning, questioning, until there is no more question. That is how to find out the truth!

* Japan Honbu Dojo Interview, February 2008

II

正義

Seigi **means correct adherence to righteousness.**

If you use the mental power of prayer to fulfill selfish desires only, the result is very bad! You might experience several accidents, or you may even develop some sort of sickness, also.

On the other hand, if this spiritual concentration and focus is used for good purposes, then it can become a type of protective mind force. In some cases, it is even possible to utilize Nature's power also.

* Japan Honbu Dojo, February 2008 and
Japan Taikai, October 2015

III

Ki energy training develops in two ways.

Ki comes naturally by training in our martial art, but there are dedicated training methods also. One method called *kiko* (standing *qigong* meditation) is available to Genbukan members at any stage of practice. But of course, at the master level there are other more secret cultivation techniques.

In my experience, certain types of ki even have the potential to assist in healing another person's body. There are varying nuances to this energy. So, sincere and honest training is required to touch another's spirit using your body, heart and soul combined with that of Nature.

PART 8

正定

SHOJO - CORRECT MEDITATION

Keep a humble and grateful heart for the universe and God. Realize the kindness allotted to you just in enjoying everyday life: normal living, simply eating, and having clothes and shelter. Do good by all your actions, and it will be returned to you. I am always amazed at the results of using this theory – so simple in its beauty. Some think it's complicated, but it's not. And, it is the key to happiness.

* Bufu "Kancho's Greetings – April, 1989

I

Some people believe that to think of "nothing" is the goal of meditation. But that's not the correct way! For one, this misguided goal is an impossible thing to do. Also, it is psychologically dangerous to give up the control of your mind to "emptiness".

In the true way of meditation, you must first clean up your heart and methodically re-correct your bad habits. After *hansei* (reflection), then real meditation can start. This is also the basis of positive contact with the subconscious mind. Consistent practice like this can even develop a defense for your heart/mind too.

* Japan Taikai, October 2015

II
魂は何でか？

What is called the *tamashii*?

The *tamashii* is the traditional Japanese term for "soul". It is a spiritual part of us made of light.

Use what I am teaching to polish your heart daily with correct meditation. Your efforts will get better results when you apply them consistently and patiently. With fortitude, the light of your *tamashii* can be polished to shine more brightly!

* Ireland Amatsu Tatara Taikai, August 2009

III

七転八起

Takamatsu Sensei always said, "Seven times down, eight times up!"

悲しみも恨みも自然の定めと思い、
唯だ不動心の悟りを得可し

Think of sadness and grudges as destiny. This means keep *fudoshin* and never give up training.

Make improvement naturally and remember: Keep going this way!

A SUDDEN EXPLOSION

While strolling on the street to get dinner one summer night, an explosion like a loud bomb shattered through the air right behind my head!

Jagged pieces of metal, up to ten centimeters long, and heavy shards of glass flew all directions for many meters. Even so, all of the pieces stopped flying and dropped to the ground only a few inches behind me. Miraculously, I was completely untouched.

I was uninjured, but another passerby was not so lucky. Unfortunately, he got impaled by some of the metal shrapnel. The projectiles pierced clean through his jacket and embedded themselves in several places in his back. The pain, force and surprise were so much that he was sent running and screaming across the street!

I forgot about supper and stayed to give a report to the policemen who arrived on the scene.

They told me that the large, electrical power transformers hanging above the street were very rusted and outdated. The entire block was at risk. So, this "timebomb" was a random accident waiting to happen. The officer said he had seen explosions like this before, and that it will definitely happen again.

This concerned me greatly because many of the children that study at the dojo go to a school on the same block. At least two of these transformers hung menacingly above the crosswalk that the children use every day. This fact was so troubling that I even offered to take up a collection and pay the city to replace them. Later, I met with an inspector and he told me that the ones next to the school were actually older than the one that exploded near me. I contacted the Office of the Mayor and was able to connect with the executive in charge of my area. I also talked to the energy company that is responsible for all of the electricity in my city. I related this story to them and explained about the children. I took pictures of the faulty equipment and convinced them to change every single transformer, including those that hung above the school.

Everything happens for a reason. The near miss taught me many things. But what was clear right away was that my life was not as important as those of the children. I'm so glad that I was able to discover a way to use *hassen tenkan*, to take a bad situation and turn it around into a positive one. This concept was taught to me by Soke, and I am constantly amazed at the results of using it.

TEACHING MARTIAL ARTS IN SEVEN COUNTRIES

In the beginning, using my passport was novel and exciting. There were new sights to see, new foods to sample and new foreign phrases to acquire. Authentic cultural experiences are always interesting.

However, the deeper purpose of my travels was to introduce and invite new members to adopt the best aspects of Japanese martial arts culture as taught by Soke.

After the honeymoon stage, it was down to business. Dispelling doubts and impressing the hearts of people that live thousands of miles away from my teacher are not always easy tasks. Of course, there are many foreign instructors who are naturally impressed and sincerely excited by the depth of what our martial arts tradition has to offer. However, it takes a special kind of person to actually humble themselves and do what is necessary to immerse into the tradition correctly.

In my experience, it took over ten years of consistent teaching and vigilance in each country to determine if that dojo-cho was truly willing to be loyal to the principals I have expounded in this book. Some people conduct themselves honestly. These virtuous few are always true to their word and unwavering in following the Genbukan rules. However, this is not universally the case.

After a decade, teachers gradually start to learn the basic skills and unique strategies that Tanemura Sensei teaches. Still, it's always important to make sure that egoism or selfishness doesn't develop unchecked. Being a dojo-cho is an honor, but with that privilege comes great responsibility.

A *shibu-cho* (regional director) is one who has *dojo-cho* and group leaders under their supervision. The final *kanji* at the end of both words, *cho*, can be equivalent to the English word "long."

Personally, I see this as representing long years of training, long hours of volunteer work and long periods of patience. In any case, after dedicating over three decades of my life, I can say with confidence that the inner rewards attained from this difficult path of helping others far outweighs any amount of growing pains.

One of the main things I tell new *dojo-cho* instructors is that their efforts should not be focused exclusively on themselves. The development of the next generation is the most important consideration. "It's not about you."

CHEATING DEATH IN SOUTH AMERICA

I've had the opportunity to share this martial art multiple times in three different South American countries. This is in addition to the other nations in North America and Europe in which I had already instructed. But, the goal of establishing dojos long-term is more about quality than quantity.

Each experience had a unique flavor. Some encounters were warm and inviting, and other experiences actually exposed me to some dangerous situations. The following story happened during a sight-seeing trip into the hinterland of one of those countries.

I had a feeling something serious was going to happen that day. So, I ordered everybody to pray for protection solemnly before we left the hotel. After several moments of silence, the four of us took up our positions in the car. I rode "shotgun," while the dojo-cho, a group leader and a translator filled the remaining positions. Then, we embarked on our journey into the wildest part of the country.

The road was long, but the company was lively. The terrain went through many changes as we passed everything from alligator-infested swamps, grasslands full of gigantic cattle and picturesque rolling hills. Not to be outdone by the highway, our destination had also promised even more amazing, nature-based tourist attractions: crystal clear lakes for snorkeling, ancient caves for spelunking and a variety of photogenic animals too numerous to list.

After some time, we finally arrived at the town center. The admission fees for each of the day's attractions were handled in the city hall and not at the nature sites themselves. This fact becomes important later.

After a quick bite to eat, we embarked on our quest deeper into the countryside. One of the passengers in the back seat was very good at interpreting into English all the questions and concerns of the other passengers.

In addition to the flora and fauna, the people in charge of each site seemed to be native to the region. Even recently, there is still tension between the groups of people who control the flow of money and the native people who do the less glamorous work.

The last site was very unique, and my words definitely do not do it justice. This attraction is defined by an ancient valley. This prehistoric area allows visitors to watch hundreds of colorful birds flying beautifully in pairs from above. This view looking down from the sky over the backs of exotic birds was unique in my experience. But I almost didn't live to see it.

The sun was going down. And, the site I described above would become totally invisible after sunset. So, on a back woods dirt road, we raced the car against the inevitable rotation of the earth.

All alone, we sped against time. The car kicked up such a dust cloud that it was getting increasingly difficult to see. Along the way, the other inhabitants of the vehicle were unrelentingly firing question after question at me. The sights and sounds of the scene were starting to overload my senses...

The ding of the dirt and pebbles kicking up under the wheels... the rumble of the bumps and vibrations of the quickly moving car... and the hazy disappearance of the orange globe peeking through the trees on its unstoppable downward path.

"STOP!" I yelled, once in English and then in Portuguese.

I had a terrible feeling and the only correct action was to immediately discontinue our forward motion. The driver followed my orders even though he had no idea why they were necessary.

Even though we had come to a complete stop, the dust was so thick that it took a few seconds for us to see the way ahead clearly. To the amazement of everyone, including me, there was a very large, fallen tree intentionally laid across the road only about two meters in front of us. – The tree trunk was so huge, and the booby trap so deliberate that I have no doubt that if we hadn't stopped, I would have lost my life!

At the beginning of the story, I explained how there are sometimes protests in certain countries to show disfavor against various policies. Clogging up this road seemed to be one of them. – After we in the car collected ourselves, gave thanks and started to drive around to avoid the obstacle, we realized that several such booby-traps had been laid on the path to the next natural attraction.

We survived them all with no further incident and even got to witness the wonderful birds who pair for life and never seem to let the difficulties in their environment slow them down.

MICHAEL, YOU WILL NOT TEST THIS TIME IN JAPAN

"Michael, you will not test this time in Japan." Tanemura Sensei remarked matter-of-factly.

"Hai, Sensei. Wakarimasu." (Yes, Sensei. I understand.) I said without reservation.

I fully accepted my teacher's decision. And, for the first time ever, though the words meant that I was being denied the chance to test for at least another year, my heartbeat remained unaffected and maintained its steady rhythm. If someone would have asked me at that moment, "Are you disappointed?" I would have sincerely answered, "I am not disappointed." Based on all the events and revelations I've experienced since 1987, I can honestly say, I completely trust my teacher.

After one of the Tai Kai's in Japan, a large group of international students was allowed to stay behind for extra training at the Honbu (Headquarters Dojo) in Saitama-ken. On the first day of training, the Grandmaster outlined the goals Soke expected us to accomplish before we headed back home. Each student was given personalized targets. However, for me, testing for Nanadan in KJJR Jujutsu did not seem to be one of them.

The days passed smoothly. We all trained with discipline and sincerity. Tanemura Sensei made sure that each person received direct teaching and helpful kuden.

Eventually, groups of students departed the country one-by-one. Gradually, I realized that I would be the last of the foreign students to leave Japan. About three days before my flight home, to my surprise, Tanemura Sensei made another announcement.

"You will test for seventh degree tomorrow, Michael!"

"Hai, Sensei. Wakarimasu." I said to him in a state of surprise. This time my heart felt warm.

After my successful examination and saying goodbye to my fellow students, the Honbu Dojo was very quiet. My last class was almost a private lesson. There was only Soke teaching, his nephew Okayasu Shihan, his son Kotaro Shihan and me. After training, Tanemura Sensei took me out to dinner. Without me mentioning it, Soke explained that the night before the announcement, he had received a sign that it was the correct time to test me. I am continually humbled by the forces of compassion that I cannot explain.

TEST IN MEXICO

As I sat high atop the Pyramid of the Moon at Teotihuacán in Mexico, I contemplated my last days as a sixth-degree black belt in Genbukan Ninpo Taijutsu. Gazing out upon this sprawling and ancient archaeological site, the air was thin. The entire time spent in and around Mexico City, I could definitely feel the altitude. For me, being almost 8000 feet above sea level took some getting used to. In my home in Milwaukee, the elevation is only about sea-level. So, oxygen is naturally more plentiful where I'm from.

It had been over a dozen, long years since my last Ninpo Taijutsu examination. And of course, during that time many important developments occurred...

My son had grown from just a little kid into a man taller than me. I had studied hard under Soke and received masterships in more than a dozen *ryuha* (martial arts traditions). And, several of my students had graduated beyond yondan (fourth-degree black belt) and achieved the Renshi level in their own right. To date, I'm very proud to say that I have six students who have passed through that grade.

Over the years, it became increasingly obvious to me that the promise of achieving the higher levels of black belt in this art is not guaranteed. Even though Soke remarks honestly that it's possible for all sincere practitioners to eventually become masters, if the instructor's heart changes for the worse, all progress is retarded. – Years of training matter. Hard work is certainly expected. But, in the end, it all comes down to "you."

Personally, I've found that the only way to truly realize what was missing is to simply keep going. To paraphrase something Soke said to me, "If your eyes are open and you reflect on your mistakes and you concentrate on the step that is in front of you, everything you need will be revealed in time."

In the heart of Mexico Distrito Federal, the steps I had to climb this time were made of modern metal and not ancient stone. It was testing day at the Mexico Taikai. After following hundreds of fellow Genbukan members up several more flights of stairs, we finally arrived in the huge training hall.

Months before at the Honbu Dojo, certain sections of my level had already been evaluated in front of the Grandmaster and Shihan. During the training in Matsubushi Town, I was ordered to perform the other more secretive aspects of the seventh-degree black belt *waza* (techniques). The final part, saved for Mexico, was still extremely rare to see and seldom shown outside of Japan.

As I repeated both the left and right side of my techniques, the altitude and weeklong *Kukishinden Happo Bikenjutsu ryuha* training prior to that moment started to catch up with me. Exertion and lack of oxygen made every technique increasingly more difficult. Even so, I kept my pace steady, my focus concentrated and my *kiai* (spirit shout) strong.

When we switched from the unarmed to the weapons portion of the test, I got a special feeling. With it, my surroundings seemed to disappear. Except for the constant awareness of Tanemura Sensei's eyes upon me, only my training partner wielding a sword existed. Everything proceeded automatically after that. I paid no attention to my breath or fatigue. And it seemed, the test was over surprisingly quickly.

Kotaro Shihan was one of the judges that day, and he remarked to me after my performance. "Michael, I could tell that you gave everything you had to give during that test!" I heartily thanked him for his help and kind words.

We are all human. – After taking four, different tests at the Taikai, my body certainly remembered all of the effort it had been asked to perform. It was an incredible experience that I will never forget. I was tired but extremely happy!

AFTERWORD

"Use Ninpo and other martial arts to build a utopia with the motto: love, generosity and peace."

−Takamatsu Toshitsugu

At the thirteenth annual USA Milwaukee Taikai, Tanemura Sensei lectured about the spiritual dimension of training in our martial art tradition. Two things were introduced as being very important to keep in mind and discover in order to make this path meaningful: *Moku Teki* (purpose) and *Shi Mei* (duty or mission).

At the age of twenty-seven, the Grandmaster received a very powerful teaching: the general purpose of every person is to contribute skillfully to the establishment of a properly functioning society, a utopia. The main three qualities inherent in such a balanced community are: sincere justice, compassionate mercy and unconditional acceptance (love). – Ten years later, Tanemura Sensei realized his own mission to teach this way of peace in every part of the world. He also began to inspire others to find and fulfill their own responsibilities and duties.

I believe that the key word here is "inspiration." – For some reason, my teacher's ability to stop any attack with only one finger and to wield a sword in beautiful arcs within a hair's breadth of my life inspires me to strive to be a better person. When I walk into an inner city classroom wearing my uniform and black belt, the children seem to be instantly more interested in what I have to say about character development.

A *kobudo* (ancient martial arts) *dojo* is one of the few institutions you'll find today wherein respecting one's elders, honoring one's family, and loyalty to one's teacher are not just hollow words. They become absolute. – True *ninpo* masters are not afraid to risk their necks to prove that they are fit to help other people. In addition, the literal balance between life and death is actually decided solely by one's degree of humility. It is no game, but it has provided me more happiness than I ever thought possible.

CHAPTER NOTES

Chapter I

i Shoto Tanemura's titles: President, Genbukan World Ninpo Bugei Federation; President, Kokusai Jujutsu Renmei / Federation; Executive Director, Japan Jujutsu Federation; Saitama Director, Japan Chinese Martial Art Federation. Shoto Tanemura's masterships:

-Hontai Yoshin Takagi Ryu Jujutsu - 18th Soke
-Hontai Kukishin Ryu Bojutsu - 18th Soke
-Gikan Ryu Koppo-Jutsu - 14th Soke
-Asayama Ichiden Ryu Taijutsu - 18th Soke
-Tenshin Hyoho Kukishin-Ryu - 18th Soke
-Amatsu Tatara Bumon & Shumon - 58th Soke
-Shinden Tatara Ryu Taijutsu - 55th Soke
-Shinden Kito Ryu Bojutsu - 55th Soke
-Bokuden Ryu Jujutsu - 15th Soke
-Itten Ryushin Chukai Ryu Jujutsu - 3rd Soke
-Chinese Martial Art Hakkesho - 5th Denjin
-Araki Shin Ryu - Menkyo Kaiden
-Yagyu Shingan Kacchu Yawara - Menkyo Kaiden
-Tenshin Koryu / Shindo Tenshin Ryu Kenpo - Menkyo Kaiden
-Kijin Chosui Ryu Daken-Taijutsu - Menkyo Kaiden
-Daito Ryu Aiki Jujutsu Yamamoto-Ha - Menkyo Kaiden
-Mugen Shinto Ryu Iai-Jutsu - Menkyo Kaiden

-Shinden Fudo Ryu Daken-Taijutsu Tanemura-Ha - Soke
-Shinden Fudo Ryu Taijutsu Tanemura-Ha - Soke
-Kukishinden Happo Biken-Jutsu Tanemura-Ha - Soke
-Togakure Ryu Ninpo Tanemura-Ha - Soke
-Gyokko Ryu Kosshi-Jutsu Tanemura-Ha - Soke
-Koto Ryu Koppo-Jutsu Tanemura-Ha - Soke

ii In Heisei year I (1989) June 19th at 7:00am, I departed from the hotel, and took the 8:30am flight on Northwest Airlines to Milwaukee, Wisconsin. During the journey we went from clear skies into fog. I saw a portion of it colored in gold. I found my eyes and heart attracted to it. Inside this, I saw a bright glow. A voice came from it telling me clearly of future events of my ryu-ha, and also about things that needed to be done. It instructed me in miraculous points, and to reinstate many Kobudo schools. I was deeply grateful to Heaven for this inspirational vision. It started me thinking of many things. At the airport, the Dojo-cho Michael Coleman was waiting for me.

-Tanemura Sensei

Chapter II

iii Gikan ryu Linage of Grandmasters: (1) Uryu Hogan Gikanbo; (2) Uryu Hogan Yoshichika; (3) Uryu Kanzui; (4) Uryu Nobuyoshi; (5) Uryu Tenkaibo; (6) Uryu Yoshitaro Hidechika; (7) Uryu Sokaibo; (8) Uryu Shinkaibo; (9) Uryu Gikaibo; (10) Uryu Gikanbo (Gikan); (11) Ishitani Matsutaro Takakage; (12) Takamatsu Toshitsugu Uoh; (13) Sato Kinbei Kiyoaki; (14) Tanemura Tsunehisa Shoto.

BIBLIOGRAPHY

Tanemura, (Tsunehisa) Shoto. *Ninpo Secrets*. Saitama:Genbukan, 1992.

Tanemura, (Tsunehisa) Shoto. *Genbukan Taijutsu Manual Vol.1*. Saitama:Genbukan, 1987.

Tanemura, (Tsunehisa) Shoto and Coleman, Michael. *Kokusai Jujutsu Renmei Jujutsu Manual*. Milwaukee: KJJR, 1999.

GLOSSARY-INDEX

ABOUT THE AUTHOR

Michael Coleman started training in martial arts in early childhood. But, his true martial arts apprenticeship didn't begin until he met Grandmaster Shoto Tanemura in 1987. Later, Tanemura Sensei started making the trek to Milwaukee and personally instructing Mr. Coleman, in 1989.

Since then, the Grandmaster has held a *Taikai* there on 20 separate occasions. Michael also flies to Japan to study with his teacher each year and in other foreign countries.

Michael Coleman's Japanese title is *Kyoshi*. He has earned a *Nanadan* (seventh degree black belt) and has also passed the special sword test, which is given only after one has mastered the physical techniques and is prepared to face the mental challenges of the art. He has taught in sixteen American states and also various foreign countries including: Brazil, Chile, Argentina, Italy, Spain and Canada.

Shibu-cho (Regional Director) is Mr. Coleman's other title, and as such he has the responsibility to bring Tanemura Sensei, as well as his *Shihan* (highest master) level students from Japan whenever possible. In addition, and as part of his ongoing duties to support any Genbukan or KJJR dojo or students who request his help, he also conducts seasonal seminars of his own.

For more information please visit www.genbukan.org & http://www.futendojo.com

Printed in Great Britain
by Amazon

80660944R00129